Ty and Pat Boyd

Ty Boyd has spent a lifetime learning the tools of the powerful communicator, tools that have made him a successful broadcaster, consultant, teacher and internationally-known professional speaker. Ty is past president of the 4,000 member National Speakers Association; a member of the Speaker's Roundtable; founder of the Excellence in Speaking Institute; winner of the three top awards in the speaking profession, the CSP, the CPAE for Platform Excellence and the "Oscar" of the National Speaker's Association, the coveted Cavett Award; and a member of the North Carolina Broadcaster's Hall of Fame. He is author of the 1991 book, **VISIONS: *From the Leaders of Today for the Leaders of Tomorrow*.**

Ty lives in Charlotte, North Carolina, with his wife and business partner, Pat. They have six children and 8 grandchildren, which has been as valuable as all their professional experience in teaching them about the need for effective communication skills.

OTHER BOOKS BY TY BOYD:

VISIONS: From the Leaders of Today for the Leaders of Tomorrow
Speaking Secrets of the Masters (co-author)
Insights into Excellence (co-author)

Additional praise for Ty Boyd and his ability to bring out the successful communicator in all of us:

"If all of us used the communication tools Ty teaches in *The Million Dollar Toolbox*, we would be more successful spouses, parents, bosses, employees and human beings. Now if Ty could just do something about my golf game."
Mike Purkey, *Senior Editor, GOLF Magazine*

"If you never talk to anyone else, you can afford to skip this book. Otherwise, it's a must-read."
William Schultz, *President, DIXIE Business, Georgia-Pacific*

"Ty Boyd is truly an expert in his field. He is a tremendously talented speaker and teacher. The passion that Ty projects while teaching and speaking is truly inspirational. The small investment of time that I spent with Ty has certainly paid huge dividends in my career."
Ray Evernham, *NASCAR Team Owner*

"Ty Boyd is one of the most powerful teachers I have ever come across. I have watched in amazement as time after time he has transformed poor communicators into good ones and good ones into masters. In *The Million Dollar Toolbox*, Ty brings his techniques and expertise to the printed page so that we can all experience the magic of effective communication."
Randy Hall, *Global Director, Training and Development*
Pfizer Animal Health

"Nobody does it better! Ty Boyd is the 'Cary Grant' of professional speaking. He is a MASTER communicator and teacher who can transform your communication skills from good to GREAT."
Dr. Tony Allesandra, Author of *The Platinum Rule* and *Charisma*

"No one is better qualified to give us new tools and improve old ones than Ty Boyd. His wisdom has impacted millions through his students."
Charles "Tremendous" Jones, *CPAE*

"I came to Ty Boyd seeking my voice; I left having regained my life. How different the world looks when I use my strength not to control, but to inspire."
Edward C. Peple, III "Troy", *President & CEO, ChainLinks Retail Advisors*

"To know and work with Ty has been an honor and a privilege. Ty is one of the truly great human beings on the planet and a speaker par excellence. I can honestly say that his Executive Speaking Institute is phenomenal—after I participated in the course some years ago, my confidence soared, my connection with the audience came alive, and my bookings and income quadrupled. He has indeed mastered the arts of teaching, communicating and being human. I am delighted he's making the powerful skills he teaches available to everyone."

Tom Feltenstein, *Chairman and CEO*
The Neighborhood Marketing Institute
Author, Motivational and Inspirational Speaker
Founder, NMI Annual Marketing War College

"My company began sending high potential employees to Ty Boyd in the early '90s. A skillful communicator, Ty helps students believe in their abilities and to carry that strength into a win-win situation for themselves and their customers. If you can't experience a one-on-one power drive, at least own *The Million Dollar Toolbox* and keep it at your right hand."
Frank Dowd IV, *Chairman and CEO, Charlotte Pipe and Foundry Company*

"Ty's pragmatic approach to the power of communication is so vital that we have all of our people at IGA Corporate take advantage of his training…with continuous refresher sessions. Ty's lifetime consistency, commitment and compassion have lifted our people to new levels of effectiveness and personal satisfaction. We are pleased that he has reduced some of his best experiences and expressions to print, which will become a desktop companion in IGA offices throughout the world."
Thomas S. Haggai, *Chairman and CEO, IGA, Inc.*

THE MILLION DOLLAR TOOLBOX

A Blueprint for Transforming Your Life and Your Career with Powerful Communication Skills

by
Ty Boyd

*With an Introduction by
Patricia Cowden Boyd*

Published by ALEXA PRESS 1-800-336-2693.

ISBN 0-9713742-0-1 (hard cover)

ISBN 0-9713742-1-X (paperback)

Photography by Jeff Carsten, Southern Light Photography, Charlotte, North Carolina

Cover design by Tracy Rozanski, Charlotte, NC

Layout by Tracy Rozanski, Charlotte, NC

Text typeface Veljovic Book 11pt

Contact Ty Boyd Executive Learning Systems
and the Excellence in Speaking Institute at
704-333-9999 or www.TYBOYD.com.

Listen
- Hold off ~~with~~ WITH COMMENTS or
QUESTIONS!!

Roadblocks
✓

NAP

3950 Las Vegas Boulevard South • 877.632.7000
Las Vegas, Nevada 89119-1006 • mandalaybay.com

CONTENTS

ACKNOWLEDGEMENTS

Ty Boyd

Seeing your life's work captured between the covers of a book is an experience that humbles me. Doubly so when you realize you could never have done it alone.

My gratitude can never be fully expressed; and the debt I owe countless others for all they've taught me can never be repaid. But let me try to identify those who enriched my life and gave me gifts I try to pass on to others, both in this book and in the coaching I'm privileged to do.

My mom, Adabelle Boyd, was the best fourth grade teacher in all the public schools of North Carolina. I had the great fortune to be in her class, and to have her as my best teacher ever throughout her lifetime. What a communicator. Listener. Coach. Admirer. Encourager. Leader. Role model. My dad, Jerman Boyd, gave me patience, a great example and an openness modeled by "never meeting a stranger."

Others have influenced my life's work, and this writing. Early in life, I met strong and influential men and women like Sandy and Bet McClamroch, Bill and Camille Stribling, Scott Jarrett, Jim and Pam Heavner, Jim and Mary Lou Babb, Wade St. Clair, and Loonis and Nan McGlohon. All broadcasters. Each an outstanding communicator who taught me by example. Add to the list my defining mentors, Charlie Cullen and Bill Gove, and my longtime friend Dr. Tom Haggai, chairman of IGA, Inc., who may be the best corporate communicator in the world.

Two groups who clearly lead in their profession have my undying thanks. The first are the thousands of members of the National Speakers Association who, though not always household names, set such high standards of communication from the platform for all to follow. I have great admiration for them. No profession works harder to make it look easy!

The second organization from which I have learned so much, Speakers Roundtable, has influenced much of what we teach in our three-day Excellence in Speaking Institutes. They are arguably the best of the best. Each has been eager to share his/her skills. Learn from Executive Learning Systems and you learn from my fellow professional speakers as well.

Finally, I have learned marvelous lessons from my students—executives, managers, community leaders, professionals and more—as well. Each leaves me a better coach, a better communicator. My next classes, and all who read this book, have more from which to learn thanks to them.

I also want to thank the organizations from all points of the globe that have trusted their best people to my care. I am humbled and most appreciative. You have been among my greatest supporters, to whom I owe much.

Finally, you would be so fortunate to know Peg Robarchek, who as collaborator has helped me capture my life's lessons for the printed page. Her genius is evident throughout this tome. She has so many more communications skills than even the most talented of us. Andrea Cooper acted as super-editor and project champion. Sheila Adams adds creativity and form to our project; Lynn Daniel keeps us all moving forward, and focused on our mission of passing on powerful communication skills to all who want them. Our entire ESI faculty contributed invaluable ideas to these pages. Thanks to Lou Solomon, Cam Marston, Anne Boyd Gellman, David Reinhardt, Evelyn Nikkel, Peter Ashley, Laura Schanz and Mike Furr. Somehow this list would not be complete without including daughter Molly Boyd, who allows us to view the world in a marvelous way through her eyes. Talk about social skills and savvy. I hope you'll meet Molly when you visit our offices or attend one of our life-changing sessions.

And then there is Pat.

Patricia Cowden Boyd, my bride, my partner, the inspiration for the teaching and coaching that have become our passion in life. You will see Pat's imprint throughout the book, sometimes with her name attached, most often not. Because nothing you see on these pages would have been possible without Pat's wisdom and insight and enthusiasm. My fondest wish for all of you is that better communication skills will help you create the kind of relationship I've been blessed to have with Pat. She is truly one in a million.

Now, I leave you to the chapters that follow. It has taken me a lifetime to learn what you can have in a few hours reading. But please don't stop with the reading. Practice is what makes these secrets come alive. Work at it the way Tiger Woods or Jack Nicklaus, Michael Jordan or Mia Hamm do. You, too, will become a world champion. There will be no stopping you.

And the ride is unbelievable!

Best wishes,

Ty Boyd, CSP, CPAE

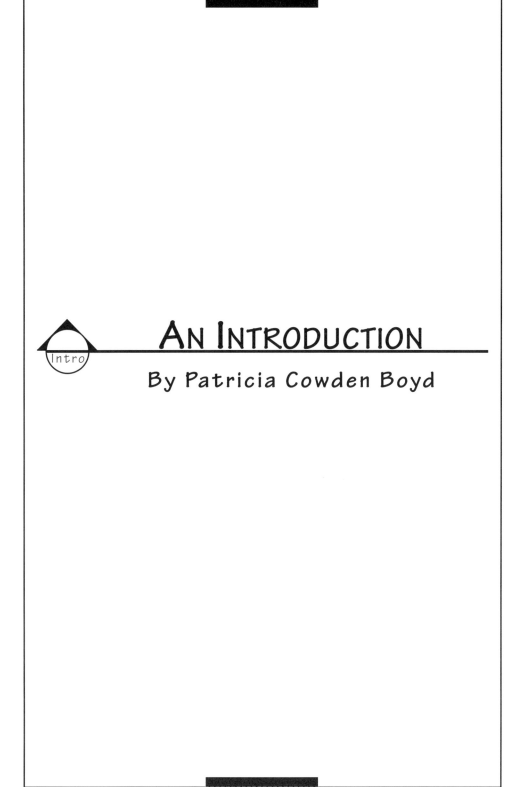

An Introduction

By Patricia Cowden Boyd

P a t r i c i a

B o y d

Few things are harder than taking center stage when you don't feel adequate to the job.

Each time we open a session of our Excellence in Speaking Institute, Ty and the rest of us see how that affects people: sweaty palms, shaky voice, fidgeting. And each time we hold our graduation ceremony, we see the miracle of people who now know they are well-equipped whenever and wherever they must take center stage, whether it's in a sales meeting, a community service opportunity, a family discussion or an auditorium full of people.

I've personally experienced that miracle. And that's one reason I was so excited when Ty and I hit upon the idea of founding ESI in 1980.

Years before that, before Ty and I ever met and became life partners, I had the opportunity to take center stage myself when I was named the Maid of Cotton. Here in the South, the national Maid of Cotton pageant was second only to the Miss America competition in prestige. The winner was designated an international spokesperson and representative for the Cotton Council of America, a heady experience for a small-town girl with a junior college education. My selection indicates I must have been presentable looking—the prettiest girl never wins—and that I could express myself well enough under pressure. Part of the competition entailed speaking to about 3000 people, and speaking was a major part of the responsibility that came with winning.

But I had nothing of substance to share about the cotton industry, and I knew it. That lack made me feel inadequate, especially when I looked out over audiences full of experts from all over the world. Being a tall redhead suddenly seemed like a very poor qualification.

I learned under fire how to overcome that feeling of inadequacy. Speaking as often as five times a day, I learned how to connect with my audience no matter how hard my knees were knocking. I learned how to practice enough that I sounded knowledgeable even when I wasn't. I learned how to smile and look people in the eye.

I didn't know it at the time, but I was learning the secrets of powerful communication.

Later, as the wife of an accomplished speaker, trainer and communicator, I kept polishing those skills. I kept listening and learning. Ty and I knew we had something, but I don't think either of us knew how powerful it was until we started teaching it to others.

When Ty was first asked by Tom Carpenter of Aetna and Rick Dyer with Apple Computer to teach public speaking skills to their employees, he wasn't crazy about the idea. But he had the time in his schedule, so he said, "Why not?" Ty watched the people in those classes walk away more confident, more capable, more powerful. Not because they were learning how to **talk** to others, but because they were learning how to **communicate** effectively with others.

That's a big distinction and the main message Ty wants you to carry with you after you've read this book: There is a world of difference between talking to others and communicating with others.

Effective communication is a million-dollar skill, a path to success in all areas of your life, personal and professional.

For more than twenty years now, Ty and I have been blessed to be a part of coaching men and women all over the world to improve their communications skills. We've been all over the U.S. and the world, coaching people from places as diverse as Russia, China, South Africa and South America. We share the tools we know work. It is our purpose and our passion.

Ty can't wait to share it with you. And he's even asked me to contribute here and there throughout the book, in short segments he calls The Coach Speaks. It's all part of the invaluable process Ty likes to call *The Million-Dollar Toolbox*.

JOURNEY TO EFFECTIVE COMMUNICATION

Ch. 1

« Effective communication skills are the path to a richer, more rewarding life. Family, friends, career—all will be enhanced when we can communicate more effectively. »

Have you ever watched your career circling the drain in front of tens of thousands of people?

It happened to me one day in the early 1970s. It was one of those moments we all have, a moment we relive over and over again, simply because it was so humiliating we never want to go through anything like it ever again.

I was at the top of my game. I'd filled in for Arthur Godfrey on the CBS network. I'd hosted a dance party show that was hotter in the Carolinas than Dick Clark's American Bandstand, emceed the Thanksgiving Day Parade for CBS-TV. During my fifteen years in broadcasting, I'd interviewed the cream: Richard Nixon, Bob Hope, Julie Andrews, Bill Cosby, Maggie Smith, Hugh Downs.

Old Big Deal had really arrived. And I'm sure I'm not the only one who's ever felt that way when life is dealing us a terrific hand.

That particular day, I was to interview Jonathan Winters for the noon talk show I hosted on WBTV, the CBS affiliate in Charlotte. Now, Winters was the comedian whose eccentric style inspired the work of Robin Williams and Steve Martin, and I was thrilled to pull celebrity duty. It was exciting to be bringing our audience such a funny, funny man.

But, as was sometimes the case, I saw the interview as my time to shine.

I sat down with the legendary comedian, known for his manic style, his offbeat characters, and set out to impress him with the wit and wisdom of Ty Boyd. I made a clever comment. I tried to one-up him with a wisecrack. I tried to beat one of the funniest men in the world at his own game.

After all, that's the way the game was played. Celebrity interviews in particular were duels, a contest of wits to see who came off looking the best. Who could get the most laughs. Who won.

That day, Jonathan Winters won.

He won by completely shutting down.

When he realized I was playing the game I sometimes played with celebrity guests—the game I believed I was being paid to play, that the public wanted me to play—he walked off the playing field. Oh, he stayed for the interview. But he didn't make a single humorous comment, didn't whip out a single eccentric character, didn't evoke a single laugh during the entire, grueling ten minutes we were on screen together.

The interview was deadly.

I was humiliated. Ready to hang up my microphone. And my humiliation only got worse as the sad truth began to sink in: I'd brought it on myself. I hadn't been interested in interviewing Jonathan Winters, in showcasing the talent of a comic genius, in providing my viewers with insights they wouldn't get anywhere else.

All I wanted was to impress them with me.

At that moment, I was a complete failure as a communicator.

At that moment, I took a giant step in my journey to becoming an effective communicator.

Encouraging the Performer

My journey began long before that miserable day in the 1970s. It began in the small town of Statesville, North Carolina, where I must've had the world's wisest parents. Jerman and Adabelle Boyd had three boys, all totally different. And they encouraged us in our differences. Bill had a keen intellect and he found himself majoring in physics at Davidson College. My middle brother, Dick, was a natural caregiver and, with their support, he became a doctor.

And then there was me.

We had horses and cattle, chickens, a goat or two, all the farmyard animals. I worked around the barnyard because Daddy didn't give us boys a choice. But my heart was never in it. Feeding the hogs was not my passion.

My heart was in entertaining others. In making 'em laugh, in being on stage. And my parents were my best audience. They laughed for me. They encouraged my strengths, just as they encouraged Bill's and Dick's. They encouraged me right onto the stage, into roles in every play put on during my junior and senior high school career. They encouraged me right into volunteering as an announcer for the local radio station at the age of fifteen.

Now, the only people listening to that show were probably my parents. But it launched me into what I thought was a career in performing, a career in show biz, a career in entertaining.

It was years before I realized I was actually in the business of communicating.

Communicating.

Dialoguing, not monologuing. I was in the business of asking questions and listening carefully to the answers, in the business of genuine interest in someone other than myself. In the business of sensitivity and empathy. And, yes, I was also in the business of making all that communication compelling, interesting—yes, entertaining.

In fact, *most of us make our living communicating in some way or another. Most of our waking hours are spent in conversations,* one-on-one or one-to-a-boardroom, sometimes one-to-a-thousand.

When was the last time you made the effort to be sure you were doing this communicating effectively?

Interested Equals Interesting

One of the times I experienced first-hand the true power of communicating instead of simply entertaining was in Santa Fe on a movie set. As a talk show host, I was invited to many movie sets to interview the stars. I don't remember the movie in this case, but I sure do remember the star—Clint Eastwood.

On screen Eastwood always played—still does—a man of few words, and he was notorious among journalists for being the same off screen. He was a non-talker, a deadly interview.

All the prodding in the world would not compel Dirty Harry to dish the dirt.

Eastwood and I, it turns out, had a mutual acquaintance. In his early years in Hollywood, Eastwood had roomed with an Olympic record-breaker and decathlon bronze medalist named Floyd "Chunk" Simmons. Now, I also knew Chunk Simmons. So instead of asking about the movie, instead of digging where interviewer after interviewer always came up empty, I asked about Eastwood's friendship with Chunk Simmons.

I hardly had to ask another question during the entire interview.

Here was a guy who didn't talk to most people and he opened right up to me. And all it took was asking a question about something I knew meant a lot to the actor. Showing a little genuine interest. Finding our common ground in Chunk Simmons, a wonderful and colorful man.

Communication genius Dale Carnegie liked to say we'll gain more friends in two hours by being interested in others than we will in two months trying to get them interested in us.

I failed that lesson with Jonathan Winters, but had begun to learn it by the time I sat down with Clint Eastwood. The more questions I asked, the less verbiage I used, the more effective the communication. I was beginning to respect the value of listening and asking questions.

The Journey To Effective Communication

Where are you on your personal journey? When you speak to others, whether to family and friends or colleagues and clients, do you:

- view it as your time to shine?
- practice one-upmanship?
- worry about impressing others?
- make entertaining others your number one goal?

Or do you:

- attempt to have a dialogue, not a monologue?
- ask questions and listen to answers?
- practice empathy and interest?

Checking Out My Toolbox

The debacle with Jonathan Winters and the moment of clarity with Clint Eastwood weren't the only defining moments on my journey to effective communications, of course.

I've also, over the years, learned to develop my own personal style by watching how other powerful speakers, including my mentor, Charlie Cullen, set themselves apart from the pack. Charlie's physical package, his personal style, was one of his most powerful calling cards; he was built like a linebacker but dressed like a peacock. He commanded attention wherever he went. From him, I learned how important it is to know exactly who I am—and to be at pains to communicate that.

I've learned the formidable power of passion. Fire in the belly for your message. Plenty of us are moved listening to the energy of a Tony Robbins or the enthusiasm of an Oprah Winfrey.

I've learned to manage my fear instead of allowing it to manage me.

I've learned to speak with my entire body—eyes, face, posture, gestures, even the clothes I wear—and not just my voice. And I've learned, by the way, to use my voice more effectively, as well.

I've learned how to plan a strong presentation. I've learned to practice, practice, practice.

But perhaps the most important thing I've learned is that this toolbox I've just described—personal style, fire in the belly, body language, voice, face, eyes, smile, preparation—this toolbox is one we've all been given.

Yes, even you.

Every tool you need to be an effective communicator is in your toolbox today.

To one degree or another, we've all been given the tools. Now it's time to learn to use them. It's time to sharpen the ones that are rusty; to get stronger in the areas where we're weakest. No matter who we are, no matter what our circumstances, it's time to learn to use that toolbox.

A Million-Dollar Skill

Why is it so important to open up our toolbox?

Because the ability to communicate effectively is the most important skill we can develop.

Let me repeat that, because it's the most important message of this book: *The number one skill of every leader, lawyer, salesperson, executive, preacher, teacher, parent and lover is the ability to effectively communicate with others.*

Are you in sales? Gotta communicate effectively. In management? Not for long, if you can't communicate well. Teaching, preaching, parenting? All call for effective communication skills. There isn't a skill you can name that is more critical to your success, to your happiness, even. And that's true no matter who you are. No matter how you spend your day. No skill I can think of is used more often, in more areas of our lives. Or causes more problems when we don't do it well.

Communication.

It's a money skill. A relationship skill. A success skill. A growth skill.

Can you tell I've got a passion for effective communication?

For more than twenty years now, my wife, Pat, and I have been in the business of conveying our passion to people all over the world. After leaving broadcasting and spending a number of years as a professional speaker, I realized there was more I wanted to do. More she and I were called to do, if you want to know the truth. So we began teaching others what we'd learned about effective communication. We founded the Excellence in Speaking Institute (ESI), and it's been the most rewarding experience we've ever had. Because we get to watch people transform themselves.

Pat and I pass on what we've learned to executives and sales associates, bank chairmen, politicians, small business owners, attorneys and doctors, representatives of nearly every calling, in every state in the U.S. and in more than 30 countries. Overwhelmingly, our alumni tell us that better communication skills improve their lives on every level, in every arena. Even when they think they're already good communicators.

Here's an example.

One of our graduates is a minister. He came to us at a time when he was considering leaving the ministry. He wasn't reaching people the way he'd expected; he wasn't making the kind of difference in people's lives that he believed he'd been called to do.

So he came to us as sort of a last-ditch effort. Next step, a new career.

He experienced three days of re-learning the critical tools he'd been using for fifteen years. At the end of the session, when we asked if anything he'd heard had helped, he said, "I'll let you know after my next sermon on Sunday."

The phone rang Sunday afternoon. Our minister friend was excited. Fired up. Said he had decided not to leave the ministry after all. Using the simple tools he'd always possessed but now knew how to use more effectively, he had experienced a huge difference when he delivered his sermon that Sunday morning. People had responded to the altar call in greater numbers than he'd ever seen after one of his sermons. People were talking about his message with enthusiasm. He had connected with his congregation, using the one tool in his toolbox that he'd been ignoring each time he stepped into the pulpit before—eye contact.

"I was always taught not to look anyone in the congregation in the eye," he said. "All of us, in seminary, were taught to

Communication : The Million-Dollar Skill

Powerful communication improves every area of your life. It's that simple. I call it a million-dollar skill, but the truth is, it is far more valuable than that. Effective communication is:

- a get-along-with-your-spouse skill
- a job security skill
- a get-that-raise-or-promotion skill
- a negotiation skill
- a sales, management, leadership skill
- a parent, lover, partner skill
- a negotiation skill
- a money skill
- a preacher, teacher, lawyer skill
- a power skill

look over the heads of the congregation.

"But you told me to look people in the eye. You gave me techniques for making everyone in the congregation feel as if I was looking directly at them, which makes each one feel as if I'm talking directly to them."

He looked them in the eye. He connected with them. He created what we call one-to-one intimacy. Simple tools. Effective communication.

He had the toolbox. He just needed some direction in how to use it more effectively.

You've got the toolbox, too. Are you ready to use it as effectively as possible? Are you prepared to open that toolbox and create greater success in every area of your life, personal and professional?

Another of our successful graduates is a petite woman in what has traditionally been a man's industry—finance. Now, this woman was as sharp as they come in the financial arena, but her size was making her easy to overlook. She was under five feet tall, weighed less than a hundred pounds. So commanding authority was an uphill struggle for her.

When she first came to us, her size had also made her appear shy. But with our coaching, she learned to carry herself effectively, to create a sense of power in the way she stood and gestured and made eye contact.

Today, she is a giant in her industry.

Effective communication.

This isn't just a wouldn't-it-be-nice-to-have skill. It's a money skill, a relationship skill, a negotiation skill, a power skill, an exchange skill.

It's a million-dollar skill.

I tell people that all the time, and I believe it. But the truth—the Truth with a capital T—goes much deeper than that. *Effective communication skills are the path to a richer, more rewarding life. Family, friends, career—all will be enhanced when we can communicate more effectively.*

Of course, maybe you already earn all the money you want. Maybe you're content without a promotion, without a higher degree of job security. Maybe you don't care if you and your spouse reach an agreement about the direction your lives are taking. Maybe motivating your neighborhood association to adopt your vision for the community doesn't interest you at all.

Or maybe you're ready for greater success in every area of your life.

Maybe you're ready to walk out of your comfort zone and become the best speaker, presenter, teacher, the best communicator you can be. When that happens, I promise, you'll suddenly find yourself being asked to take leadership positions. You'll find people turning to you when they want guidance or action or inspiration. You will find that every area of your life is enriched, is more satisfying, both professionally and personally.

That is a promise.

When I interviewed Gloria Steinem, she said something I've never forgotten about the power of effective communications skills: "It's the fastest way to be recognized. You will be singled out and carried on the shoulders of others, all the way to the top."

Come on, open your toolbox. Let's get busy.

INVENTORY YOUR TOOLS

« All of us have every tool, every talent, every skill we need to be an effective communicator. »

I know what you think. I know because during 20 years of teaching others and hearing their innermost thoughts, I've learned that we all think the same thing.

I'll never be that good—not in a million years.

She's got better skills than I do.

He's a natural.

Her case is different—she's got talent.

That's the voice of fear and insecurity. Don't listen to it. It'll lie to you every time.

All of us have every tool, every talent, every skill we need to be an effective communicator. Every tool. Every talent. Every skill. Born with 'em. You, me, Larry King and the mechanic who can never quite explain why that funny sound under your hood is going to cost you $300. All of us, proud owners of a full toolbox.

Now, granted, some of us are blessed with a little more of one tool than another. Some of us God gave a magnificent voice. The rest of us, nobody's gonna tell us we sound like James Earl Jones because it just ain't so. (Or if it is, and you're reading this book you've obviously already figured out what I'm getting at: God didn't give one dog everything.) But if you don't have a million-dollar voice, you may have a passion for your topic so great you can't begin to put a dollar value on it. You may listen better than anyone except Larry King. (He doesn't sound like James Earl Jones, either; but, brother, can he listen!) You may carry yourself with authority without even knowing it.

All tools were not created equal. No doubt about *that*.

But by the time you work your way through to the end of this book, you'll know how to bring your weakest skills up a notch or three. You'll know how to harness your own personal talents and put them to work for you. You'll find your unique combination of skills and polish that powerful authenticity.

If you work at it, you will improve. If you work at it, you will be a better communicator when you finish this book than you are today.

More important than that, however, if you make a commitment to becoming a lifelong learner, you will be a far more powerful communicator in two years than you are today. You'll grow some more in the two years after that. You'll build on the skills in your personal million-dollar toolbox.

A Roadmap to Transformation

Here's how the book works. Each chapter covers a particular communication skill. I'll talk about how it works and why. You'll hear how others have used the tool to their advantage, or overcame their blocks to using the tool.

In each chapter, you'll also find specific practice tools, or a checklist to keep you on track, or a segment I like to call *The Coach Speaks*, with insights and guidance from my bride and partner, Pat. Those sections will help put the lessons of each chapter to work for you.

Of course, you can simply read the book and count on soaking up a little of this stuff through osmosis. And some of it you surely will; some of it might actually make a marginal difference in your presentation skills, your sales pitch, your ability to persuade your spouse or neighbor or town council members. And that's fine, if you're willing to settle for the tip of the iceberg.

The second choice is this: *Make a commitment to use this book as a workbook, a lesson plan for taking giant leaps of progress. A roadmap to transformation.*

You'll find, as Gloria Steinem predicted in the interview mentioned in the first chapter, that people soon will be carrying you on their shoulders. Your sales figures will grow. Your children will listen to you more, and learn from you. The management team will follow your lead more often. People will seek you out as a friend, a confidant, an advisor. You will find yourself taking over the corner office. If you can dream it, you can achieve it.

And the only thing that will have changed is that you have become a *master communicator.*

Ready?

Okay, let's rummage through the toolbox.

The Tools

Let's see, what have we got here?

To start, you've got some good, solid tools, the basics—a voice, a smile, eyes, gestures, body language. You've got a message. You've got two good ears and we're going to learn to use them better.

Believe it or not, you've also got your own personal style.

And you've got fear. That fear of standing up in front of a group and opening your mouth. We've all got it. After forty-plus years of making a living with my voice, I've still got it.

Fear. Even that's a tool you can use.

Briefly, let's look at each one of our tools. Then we'll move on and devote a chapter or more to learning how to put each of these tools to work.

Personal Style: Are we going to use our cookie cutter and stamp out a Tom Brokaw, an Oprah Winfrey, a Jay Leno? No. We're going to look at the wide range of individual styles and give you some pointers for uncovering your personal style, the style that is most natural for you. What works for you and what doesn't. We'll look at the traits most successful communicators share and give you pointers for incorporating them into your style. And we'll point out the major distractions that get in the way of anybody's effectiveness.

Audience Connection: This is the lesson that eluded me for years, and we're going to get it right out front so you can begin to benefit right away. If all you're doing is speaking, you're only doing half the job. *This book is about communicating, and that means connecting with your audience.* It might be a sea of expressionless faces or a single pair of piercing eyes. Whoever your audience, learning to connect with it is perhaps the single most critical factor in becoming a successful communicator. Forget your ego, forget your needs. *Connect with your audience and you will succeed.*

Listen: Next, you'll learn how to listen not only with your ears, but with your eyes. You'll learn how to pick up cues and signals from your audience, techniques for drawing information out of them. You'll learn the power of silence. How good are your listening skills? Let's work on making them better.

Using Your Body Effectively: If you're only speaking with your voice, you're shutting the lid on more than half your best God-given tools. What constitutes effective eye contact? What messages are you sending with your clothing, your posture, your gestures and facial expressions? An effective communicator is an entire package. But society and the professional community and our own fear have saddled us with a bodyguard of sorts, a set of restrictions that stifle the natural expression of our enthusiasm and our authentic self. In this chapter, we're going to help you fire that bodyguard.

Voice: This is the one tool most of us think of when we consider making a presentation of any kind. Surprisingly, studies have shown it is one of the least significant in terms of the entire package that is your message. Nonetheless, you can sharpen this tool. We'll look at vocal variety, breathing, projection, diction, enunciation, dialects, non-words—that's a biggie—and more.

The Promise of Transformation

I can't give you guarantees that you'll make a million dollars a year as a professional speaker after you read this book. But I can make this promise: if you put the tools to work, you will change and your circumstances will change.

If you are diligent and consistent in using the tools:

- you'll know how to improve your weakest communication skills;
- you'll know how to harness your own personal talents and put them to work for you;
- your personal relationships will improve;
- people will follow your lead more often;

Organizing your Presentation: The time you spend preparing your presentation is an investment in power. This chapter will present you with a number of simple but effective ways to prepare a cohesive presentation, one that delivers listeners to the destination you have in mind—whether you're making a presentation to the board, the Rotary or the teenager who isn't quite as ready as she thinks to borrow the keys to the car.

Owning the Territory: Getting comfortable in front of your audience is as simple as owning the territory. You'll learn sure-fire techniques for setting yourself at ease every time you walk into a strange setting, beginning before you even walk into the room. This chapter reveals my second-favorite mantra, a simple tool that every great presenter uses.

The Hostile Audience: The unfriendly audience sometimes comes with the territory. But you can learn how to take back your power from that person or people in the audience, how to disarm them, how to win them over, how to diffuse even the most difficult of circumstances.

Taming Your Fear: In this chapter, we tackle the monster we all dread most. Fear. You'll learn how to shine a light on your fear so brightly it no longer has power over you. This chapter is about more than tips and techniques; it's the main playing field for that transformation we mentioned earlier. *Because when you learn to tame your fear, you learn that you are capable of anything.* Anything. If you can envision it, you can accomplish it. We'll back it all up with the stories of others who have been crippled by fear, nervousness, anxiety, uneasiness—and how

- you will continue to grow as a communicator as long as you are committed to using the tools in your toolbox;
- people will seek you out as a friend, a confidant, an advisor;
- you will begin to operate out of confidence, not fear;
- you will enjoy every aspect of your life more;

- you will find your personal passion in this life, and have the opportunity to share it with others.

These may seem like extravagant fringe benefits. But I've seen them materialize over and over again for those who are willing to simply use, on a daily basis, the tools in their toolbox.

they learned to turn it into an ally. An ally we call energy.

Silencing the Be Perfect Demon: So much of our fear comes from a little demon inside us that tells us we must Be Perfect. We'll talk about the vast difference between being the best you can be versus being driven by the need to Be Perfect, between attainable excellence and impossible perfection.

Energy: Or passion; enthusiasm; fire in the belly. Energy is all the positive emotions we bring to the task. And some are astounded to learn that energy can be the flip side of fear, fear turned on its head. You can learn how to take the adrenaline rush of fear and transform it into power whenever you have the floor. You'll hear from people who have seen first-hand that, without the energy born of passion or even fear, their presentations were not as effective as they might have been. "Energy" is my personal mantra. I'm betting it will be yours, too.

There you have it—an inventory of the toolbox that can lift you from wherever you are now to the level of master communicator. Tools of transformation for your career and for your life. And I must warn you, I do not make that claim lightly. If you put these tools to work, you can change from the inside out. Your outlook on yourself and others will shift.

Personally, professionally, you will *soar.*

The Coach on Your Shoulder

coach
speaks

Pat Boyd believes the real power to enhance your skills as a communicator comes when you create your own personal communication coach.

"Once you've acquainted yourself with the tools in your toolbox," she says, "that coach is always there, sitting on your shoulder. Not to nag you or criticize you, but to encourage and remind and cheer you on. Take the coach on your shoulder with you wherever you go."

DISCOVERING YOUR AUTHENTIC STYLE

« All effective communicators have a certain style. They use their tools in a way that establishes them as unique. »

You've had a glimpse into the Toolbox. You've heard—maybe you even halfway believe—that you've got the same tools as Rush Limbaugh or Bob Costas or Diane Sawyer. Maybe.

But that's not who you are, right? You're not Billy Crystal yukking it up at the Oscars or John McCain inspiring loyalty and conviction on the campaign trail.

You're you.

And although we're going to do the best we can to help you become as effective as John McCain or Katie Couric, we're not out to turn you into them. Learning to use your personal toolbox is not a cookie-cutter process. We're here, instead, to scrape away all the veneer. To reveal the essential you. And in that way, you become the most powerful communicator you can be.

Yes, you can become as effective as any of the people just mentioned.

All effective communicators have a certain style. They use their tools in a way that establishes them as unique.

Effective communicators use their voice in their own particular way. The voice of Harry Carey defined baseball for millions of fans. And can anybody over a certain age forget the inimitable way Jack Benny had with the simple word, "Well!" Or, for a later generation, the way comedian Steve Martin conveyed volumes with the ordinary phrase, "Well, excuse me!" Benny was understated, crisp, controlled. Martin was exaggerated, bold, teetering on the edge of complete lack of restraint.

And just in case you still aren't convinced how much weight individual style carries, even former President Ronald Reagan had his own special version of "Well."

Effective communicators have signature mannerisms—Carson's golf swing; the jaunty cigar that punctuated FDR's equally jaunty smile at a time when the world was engulfed in fear and chaos; Bill Clinton's pursed lips when he wants to convey how profoundly he's moved; the smirk George W. Bush had to eliminate in order to win the 2000 Presidential election.

Effective communicators have a certain delivery style or a way of carrying themselves or a way of relating to their audiences. The best of us write our personal style all over every encounter we have with an audience, whether it's an audience of one or one hundred.

Does that mean you need to sit down and study Martin Luther King Jr. with an eye to adopting his most powerful style imprints?

Of course not. But it is time to begin discovering your own personal style. The style that comes most naturally to you. The style that taps into your strengths, strengths you can build on.

In addition, it's also time to zero in on the quirks in your personal style that limit your effectiveness, that turn listeners off, that inhibit your power to teach or persuade or lead. Those are parts of your personal style, too; but they're parts you can work to eliminate or downplay.

Teaching, Preaching and Prodding

We could spend a lot of time identifying certain styles, dissecting those styles, putting them under the microscope, even encouraging you to adapt some elements from this style or that. And in a broad sense it can be helpful to realize that there are certain identifiable types of presenters or communicators. But we're not going to spend too much time here. Because this isn't about creating a new generation of Ty Boyds—or Jesse Jacksons or Elizabeth Doles.

But let's take a few minutes to review some broad-sweep styles, because it may help you to understand the variety of effective ways in which others—and you--relate to audiences large and small. It may help you get a handle on an approach you can begin to cultivate.

The Teacher: Self-explanatory. This type of presenter conveys information. Carl Sagan comes to mind. One of my favorites is Doris Kearns Goodwin, the presidential historian whose warm smile and approachable way of conveying her vast knowledge have made her an impressive expert on TV news. Or Oprah Winfrey, who became a spiritual teacher for so many with the genuine passion she brought to the task of feeding us information that fed our spirits. The teacher may or may not be bringing original information to the table; s/he may merely pull together existing information and present it in a clear and compelling way, in a way that convinces the listener to put that information to work.

The Persuader: This person is in the business of getting us to buy—a product, a belief, a vision for what could be. Billy Graham and Martin Luther King Jr. have been the ultimate persuaders of our generation. Jesse Jackson is another. They bring great passion and conviction to their message, usually a message of the heart. These people bare their souls for us, and in doing so, enable us to connect with them in a powerful way.

The Prober: Have you ever watched Mike Wallace at work on "60 Minutes"? He's the master at digging, prodding, uncovering thoughts or feelings or information none of the rest of us expected. Using a completely different personal approach, Barbara Walters does the same thing. In a somewhat different format, John McLaughlin of PBS's "McLaughlin Group" uses this style to invigorate dialogue among his opinionated guests, to stir things up and keep them interesting. And on CNBC's "Hardball", Chris Matthews uses the same confrontational style with the addition of a ready smile and a softer ego. Contrasting McLaughlin and Matthews is a marvelous study in just how broadly the same basic style can vary and still be highly effective. This style calls for one who is inquisitive and intuitive; and often, one who doesn't mind being rebuffed from time to time.

The Humorist: More than just the stand-up comedian fits in this category. This person's ultimate goal may be to provide information, to persuade or to lead, but what marks his or her style is the way humor colors—and often dominates—the presentation. We might all think of Whoopi Goldberg or Billy Crystal at the Academy Awards. But have you ever seen Chef Emeril Lagasse, who uses humor to make his cooking show wildly popular with men and children—even truck drivers and firemen love his irreverence and self-deprecating humor. Remember Keith Olbermann, the dry-witted announcer who made ever-more lucrative moves from ESPN to MSNBC and then to the Fox network? Chris Berman also made a name for himself with his humor at ESPN. Humor works. It disarms. It grabs attention.

The Conversationalist: Is there a more effective interviewer and announcer than Bob Costas? He involves us by engaging in intimate conversation with whomever he interviews. He doesn't grill, he doesn't preach, he simply employs every

Style Checklist

Most of us don't identify our styles overnight. It requires experimentation, a willingness to try different things. If you'll use this book as a workbook and put the suggestions to work, your personal style will begin to emerge.

In the meantime, here's a checklist to keep in mind:

- What mannerisms do you unconsciously use?

- Do you tend to speak more formally, or more conversationally?

- Do you illustrate your point with jokes or anecdotes? Or is your style to rely more on facts and figures, charts and graphs?

- Is your strength in boiling down complex information into bite-sized chunks people can understand easily?

- Are you comfortable sharing your personal experiences?

- Are you comfortable with confrontation?

- Do you find that people laugh easily when you share a story?

- Which is more comfortable to you, one-on-one conversation or one-to-a-crowd?

Your answers will begin to tell you whether you are best suited to being the Teacher, Persuader, Prober, Humorist, Conversationalist or Storyteller. But remember, your style will evolve as you learn to use all the tools in your toolbox. Trying to force yourself into a certain style may shut the lid on tools you don't know you have it in you to use. So be open.

Let your style discover you.

single tool of the excellent conversationalist—active listening, eye contact, sincere interest in the other person and the topic.

The Storyteller: This presenter communicates through the powerful use of stories—anecdotes, parables, examples from real life. Medical intuitive Carolyn Myss, whose lecture series and taped presentations are highly sought after by those interested in alternative medical practice and spirituality, knows how to simplify complex theories by giving examples or telling true stories that demonstrate her ideas. I'm a big fan of this style myself, because the storyteller has the opportunity to hit each of us where we live—through our emotions, our intellect, our senses. All in the same story. Stories have universal appeal. If you doubt it, study the work of mythologist Joseph Campbell, who analyzed the powerful way in which mythology taps into our shared experiences. Experiences so common they have become archetypes. This is the power of Carolyn Myss and sportscaster Gary McCord and others. This is the power of storytelling.

There you have it. The Teacher, the Persuader, the Prober, the Humorist, the Conversationalist, the Storyteller. Each style so distinctive. Each powerful in its own way. And each growing even more powerful when it blends the techniques and tactics of the other styles. The storyteller who uses humor; the conversationalist who probes for deeper insights; the teacher who persuades by supporting her position with personal anecdotes.

Objective Feedback

Identifying your personal strengths and weaknesses begins with objective feedback. You can get that feedback a number of ways.

Do you have a friend with a camcorder? Ask to be videotaped the next time you're speaking to a group. Or give a few presentations just for the camera. Then study the tape, using the checklists in this chapter as your measuring stick. Ask friends and family for feedback.

Be especially honest with yourself as you consider the Ten Deadly Distractions. Remember, you can't eliminate a problem if you pretend it doesn't exist.

Don't have a friend with a camcorder? Rent one. Or, just to get your feet wet, try an audio tape.

Join Toastmasters. Most communities have regular meetings of this organization. Both the feedback and the regular opportunity to present before a group are invaluable.

Few of us are purely one style or another. But most of us have strengths in one arena or another. Find your personal strengths. Gain a sense of your personal comfort zone. Identify your personal style and you will have boosted your effectiveness as a communicator tenfold. Or more.

Naming Our Targets

Now that we've taken a look at the most common styles among successful communicators, let's zero in on some specific areas in which we can all make improvements. Let's look at the key traits of effective communicators; then we'll talk about the ten distractions that lessen our effectiveness.

At every Excellence in Speaking Institute we offer, we ask attendees what traits they see again and again in effective presentations, whether it's the President's State of the Union address or their spouse's ultimatum when the sixteen-year-old breaks curfew. Again.

Every time we ask the question, the answers are the same. There are never any surprises.

What that tells me is that we know exactly what effective communicators do. And once we bring that awareness forward, we can then take action to adopt those traits ourselves. Or polish them a little if they aren't as strong as they could be. What we can name, we can develop.

Let's look at the list.

They have inner fire. Passion for their message. Energy. Good communicators care about what they're saying. How much do you care? Are you mailing it in, or does your message light a fire within you? If not, how can you expect to ignite a fire in others? We'll talk, in Chapter Fourteen, about how to fan that spark.

They speak with authority. They are well-prepared and well-organized. Knowledgeable about their topic. Focused on the message. Notice how this one ties in to the previous trait. Hard to have real passion for a subject you don't know much about. Tough, too, to gather enough knowledge to become an authority in some area without either having or developing a certain passion for it. If you aren't as effective as you'd like to be, is it because you haven't yet hit on the right message?

They connect with the audience. Also referred to as charisma. Our perception is that charisma is something inborn, something we either have or we don't. But I've learned, in more than 40 years in the business of communicating, that charisma is something each of us can develop. The ability to connect with the audience, whether it's your boss or your board or your spouse, is something each of us can learn to do, simply by using the tools we already have more effectively than we're using them today. We'll start that process in the next chapter.

They tell a good story. There's that storytelling thing again.

They use their voices well. They can project. Their voices are colorful, filled with what I call vocal variety. Their diction and enunciation are good. They're making the most of their particular God-given talent.

Now I'd like to add one of my own:

They are vulnerable. Vulnerable. Hmm.

My psychologist friends have to help me with this one. The actor in me is so strong it isn't always easy to allow myself to be genuinely vulnerable. The actor is always being somebody else, unlike the performer, who is simply using the actor's tools to be a more effective communicator. The actor is still behind the mask; the performer is putting him- or herself on the line.

There's certainly a place for the actor. But the thing that draws people to us is not our perfectness, not our plasticness, but our vulnerability.

Am I willing to let you see who I really am? Am I willing to let you see my frailties, my humanness? Am I willing to put myself on the line for something I believe in passionately? Powerful speakers who can be vulnerable on the platform, not perfect, not always the hero, not always totally in charge are the ones who are most powerful. It has been described as "being private in public."

Let's look at some examples (storytelling works in written communication, too).

John McCain. In the 2000 race for the Republican Presidential nomination, the American public embraced this man because he was willing to show them his emotional scars. When he talked about his harrowing experiences as a POW in Vietnam, we listened. We cared. We opened our hearts to him. Likewise, when he spoke with passion about reforming the way politics works in the U.S., many in this country were swept up in his enthusiasm. Especially when they learned that his passion had grown out of his own mistakes.

John McCain was willing to be vulnerable, to bare his soul to the American public. And the American public loved him for it.

Many of us, especially the men among us, have been trained to believe that we give away our power when we allow our emotions or our imperfections to show through. "Never let 'em see you sweat" is the macho mantra. That may work on the football field or the battlefield. But it doesn't work when our sincere goal is effective communication.

We never lose power when we use enthusiasm, emotion, intensity.

Certainly when we become vulnerable there is always the possibility of being hurt or taken advantage of. That's the nature of being vulnerable. But the rewards are so great that

Checklist for Effective Communicators	
Effective communicators:	**Ineffective communicators:**
• Have a passion for their message	• Ramble
• Speak with authority, are well-prepared	• Speak in a monotone
• Connect with the audience	• Appear to know very little about their topic
• Tell a good story	• Show no energy, no passion
• Use their voices well	• Use too many non-words
• Are vulnerable	• Exhibit poor eye contact
	• Pace or wander or fidget
	• Use profanity or questionable humor
	• Lack preparation
	• Are poor storytellers

good communicators will risk it in order to achieve effective communication.

Who else makes vulnerability work for them?

How about Oprah Winfrey? This woman is never afraid to let us see how moved she is by the guests on her show. When they tell her why they think their adoptive mother is the greatest woman in the world, her eyes fill with tears. In fact, every topic she brings to the show is a reflection of what stirs her spirit, what matters deeply to her. Children battling illness, real people whose everyday actions are heroic, families struggling with trauma and betrayal and loss—Oprah Winfrey tells us what is in her heart every day she broadcasts a show.

The result? She is the most influential and powerful woman in broadcasting today, period.

And the most significant tool in her box is her willingness to open up and give us a glimpse into her heart. Her vulnerability is a cornerstone of her power.

Inner fire. Preparation. Connection. Storytelling. Voice. And vulnerability.

They're in your toolbox today. And as we move through the book, we'll talk more about each of them. We'll train you on using each of them more effectively than you do today.

Developing Charisma

Think charisma is magic you're born with? In some cases, probably. But it can be developed. Because charisma isn't what most of us think.

Charisma isn't about shining a spotlight on me so you fall for my charm. That, in fact, is the kiss of death to charisma.

The secret to charisma is making others feel special about themselves. It is about setting aside ego long enough to trigger a passion in someone else. It's about focusing attention and genuine interest on others.

And we can all learn to do that. We can all learn to shine the spotlight on the people we are talking to. We can all learn to focus on our audience, whether it is an audience of one or one thousand. That'll be the subject of our next chapter, and the first step toward developing your personal charisma.

Other tools for charisma will follow in subsequent chapters on listening skills, facial expressions and the power of effective eye contact. Each is found in the toolbox of the charismatic communicator.

The Ten Deadly Distractions

The other side of the coin, of course, is how often we shoot ourselves in the foot with our own actions, our own limitations, our own choices when we're trying to communicate.

Just as we ask ESI attendees what traits they see in effective speakers, we also ask them what distracts them when they're trying to listen to someone speak or present. We ask them what detracts from the message. Once again, the answers are consistently the same.

We've identified **Ten Deadly Distractions.** Let's look at them.

- Rambling
- Speaking in a monotone
- Appearing to know very little about their topic
- Showing no energy, no passion
- Uh, using a lot of, well, m-m-m, non-words, you know
- Exhibiting poor eye contact
- Pacing or wandering or fidgeting
- Using profanity or questionable humor
- Lack of preparation
- Poor storytelling skills

Now, let's be honest. We all do some of these to some extent at some time or another. We ramble because we haven't thought through what we want to say, or because we don't know enough about the subject to fill the time we've been allotted. We don't look people in the eye or our enthusiasm for our topic doesn't come through in our voice or we pace and fidget because we're nervous or afraid. They're all tied together.

And all of them can be solved.

In fact, all of them can be solved by building on the strengths we already have. The strengths identified by our ESI attendees as the traits of effective communicators.

Every item on our list of distractions can be matched with one of the strengths in our previous list.

So now we know what we have to do. We know where we want to grow, no matter what our personal style.

Let me tell you about one of our ESI alums, Lou Solomon.

When Lou first stood up to share at ESI, she looked like a sweet, solemn nun. Subdued, smiling shyly, her hands clasped in front of her, she wouldn't have surprised any of us if she'd started leading us in prayer.

Now at the time, those were her shortcomings as a presenter. Her reserved demeanor made it tough for her to fire people up. She wasn't allowing her passion for her topics to rise to the surface. But over the course of our three days together, Lou learned to allow her face to light up, to bring fire to her voice, to loosen her backbone and unclasp those hands.

Now, Lou still has a sincerity and subtlety about her, but she's learned to turn those distractions into assets. Today, she's a powerful presenter.

In fact, she's so powerful, she's become one of our ESI faculty members.

You can make that kind of turnaround, too. I promise you, it's doable. No matter what your level of skill today as a communicator, I can guarantee that if you use this book as a workbook, if you make a commitment to sharpening the tools you already have, you will be a noticeably more effective communicator.

That's worth repeating: *You will be a noticeably more effective communicator.* Often, dramatically more effective.

And maybe even more significant than that: You will enjoy it. You will enjoy presenting.

You'll also enjoy the benefits that come with it. The promotions, the better relationships, the boost in your self-esteem. Oh, yes, and the money.

Afraid that'll never apply to you? Afraid, period?

That's okay. We'll take care of that in Chapter Twelve.

But up next, let's start our work on our charisma quotient. The first step may surprise you.

Personal Inventory

For someone as talented as Ty, it may seem easy to say we've all got the tools. But let's face it, most of us aren't a hundred percent in all areas.

If you're like me, you sometimes think you'd be happy to hit forty percent in some of those areas Ty just outlined. Am I right?

Let's look now at your own personal inventory and see if we can identify where you'll want to make improvements, and where you have strengths to build on. Take the time to ask yourself the following questions. Answer them in writing, because I believe you'll be surprised how much your answers change with time and practice.

- Do you feel comfortable making certain types of presentations, but not others? If so, what makes the difference? Are you comfortable making a sales pitch, but not reporting to the board on sales figures? Can you perform Hamlet, but freeze up when it's time to recount a personal story at a party? Your answers to these questions may give you clues to your personal style. By looking back at the styles Ty outlined, can you see that you are more comfortable teaching rather than storytelling? Persuading rather than probing?

- How does fear affect you when it's time to make a presentation? Can you recall your worst experience in making a presentation? What happened? What was the fall-out? Once you understand how and when fear controls you, you are ready to tackle that fear.

- How do you feel when you make a presentation to a group? Physically? Emotionally?

- When was the last time someone said, "Did you hear what I said?" or "That's not what I said at all!" How often do you get signals such as those that the lines of communication have broken down between you and someone else?

- What do you do with your hands when you make a presentation?

- How often do you 'wing it' when it's time to make a presentation?

As you work your way through the rest of the book, your answers to these questions will mark the spots where you need to strengthen your tools.

Ch. 4

CHARISMA, PART ONE : PUTTING THE AUDIENCE CENTER STAGE

« If they ain't listening,
I ain't communicating. »

Remember that stinging moment I experienced on camera with Jonathan Winters? Those were the days when I thought success was as simple as entertaining others, before I came to understand that it takes two to communicate. As long as I was talking, as long as I was center stage, I thought I was communicating.

Eventually, I learned there is a big difference between monologuing and dialoguing.

I can monologue whether anybody's listening or not. I can run on and on long after everybody in the audience has excused him- or herself and made a run for the break room. I may be an Olympic-gold monologuer, but that doesn't mean anybody's listening. And if they ain't listening, I ain't communicating.

That, friends, is monologuing.

Then there is dialoguing.

Talking **with** someone, not **to** someone. Getting the message across. Connecting with members of the audience. *Connecting.*

One of the most powerful tools you have for connecting with your audience is to focus on that audience. Think about the individuals who showed up to listen to you. Forget yourself, your ego, your needs. Think instead about serving the audience, about discovering who they are and what you can do for them during the time you have with them.

Consider each talk you make a dialogue, not a monologue.

Of course, having a good talk with a stranger isn't always easy. So the first step toward powerful dialogue is to get to know your audience.

Do Your Homework

Getting to know the audience begins long before I show up on the podium.

In most cases, we have plenty of time to get to know the members of our audience. Sometimes months, certainly weeks and at least days. We are rarely called upon to deliver a message to an audience of any type without at least some opportunity to get to know them first. And with today's technology, we can learn almost everything but their finger-prints.

Research your audience. Go to the Internet, where the information available to you is virtually, if you'll pardon the pun, limitless. Go to the library. Read the local newspaper and ask for trade association publications. Immerse yourself in their language, their culture. Find out what bothers them and what gets their heads nodding in identification, in agreement.

I want as many details as I can put my hands on about the members of my audience. How old are they? What kind of jobs do they hold? Is religion a factor? What are their politics? Who are their competitors? What burning issues affect their industry, their lives, their communities? How much do they already know about my topic?

I also like to find out who previous presenters were and call them about the setting, the people, the pitfalls awaiting me. Ask for the names of individuals who will be in the audience and interview them before you go. Prepare a few key questions and request a half-hour of their time by phone, on a day and time convenient to them. Let them tell you what kind of people you'll be meeting; how those people feel about your subject; what their questions and concerns will be.

Can you see the value of having that kind of information, not just to grease the skids the day of your presentation, but as an aid to preparing your presentation? Can you see the value of not being blindsided by their doubts or biases? Can you see the value of having time to tell them exactly what they need and want to hear, instead of having to rely on your gut instincts to see you through?

Getting to know the audience is something I do long before I get to the meeting site.

Then, and only then, do I prepare my presentation.

Can you see how that also helps you combat the apathy that can result from giving the same speech one too many times? If I tailor my presentation to a specific audience, I'll never give the same talk in the same way twice. I've found it's impossible to get bored when I'm working with fresh material each time I begin my dialogue with the audience.

Not Selling Out, Buying Into

The first time people hear me suggest that we tailor our presentations to our audience members, some folks get uneasy. They wonder if I'm telling them to change their message to suit a particular audience. So I'd like to stress that is not what I'm suggesting at all.

We'll never be all things to all people. This is not about giving away our principles, our personhood, our authority or our convictions. It's about widening the group of people with whom we're effective by opening the door for communication. It's about knowing who I'm speaking to so I can speak in a way the listener can hear.

You know, if I speak Japanese to a roomful of Hispanic entrepreneurs, I'm not likely to be very effective in my communication. If I speak Harvard to a group of West Virginia coal miners, I'm not going to be very effective. If I speak Christianity to a group of Muslims or Good Old Boy to a group

Checklist for Researching Your Audience	
• Go to the Internet for information on the company, industry, area of interest	• Talk to insiders
	• Pin down details on age, politics, the competition, the burning issues affect their industry, their lives, their communities
• Go to the library	
• Read the local newspaper	
• Ask for trade association publications	• Find out how much they already know about your topic
• Immerse yourself in the language, the culture	• Ask previous presenters about their experiences

of female accountants...well, you get the idea.

If I speak above or below or with disregard for what they know and who my audience is, I will lose them. Because there is no such thing as a captive audience. *Any member of any audience is free to tune me out as soon as he or she decides I have nothing to offer.* They can daydream, they can make notes for their next business meeting, they can read that report the boss passed on yesterday, or just pass the time critiquing the clothes and hair of everyone else in the audience—and me, as well.

Help! I'm tanking!

If you listen to your audience, sooner or later you're going to hear what you don't want to hear: You've lost 'em.

They're restless, stirring about, whispering to one another instead of listening to you. The signs are impossible to ignore **if you keep your focus on the audience.** If you listen to them, they'll tell you when something isn't working.

And if something isn't working, something's gotta change. And it won't be the audience. You're in charge of the situation and you're the one who'll have to adjust.

When you're losing the audience, it's time to shake 'em up and there are countless ways to do that.

CHANGE VOLUME. Be loud if you've been soft, soft if you've been loud.

CHANGE PACE. Speed things up or slow things down.

BE COLORFUL, NOT PASTEL. People today are accustomed to being stimulated all the time. We are responsible for keeping their attention and words alone won't do it. So we must excite people the same way in our presentations. We have no license to be black and white or pastel in our presentations. We must be colorful, exciting, energized and entertaining. Yes, that means using visual aids effectively in our presentations; but mostly it means we must be colorful ourselves. We'll talk more about that in Chapters Six and Eight.

DISRUPT THE PATTERN. Storytellers call this "creating a trainwreck." Tell a funny story, ask a question, assign a group activity, seek feedback. If all else fails, take a short leg-stretcher break.

You must change gears in order for them to change gears.

Remember, the enemy of a great presentation is monotony. And it's not that one person is monotonous and another isn't. We all become monotonous. And it's our responsibility to determine whether it's in our energy, pace, cadence, gestures or movement. If any or all of those become predictable we will become monotonous.

And if you think that doesn't affect your effectiveness, try the little exercise called *Tuned Out* on page 48.

But even the most tuned-out audience can be won over with the tools we're talking about in this chapter. It sounds so simple, and it is. So simple it often never occurs to us: *Focus your attention and your energy and your interest on connecting with the audience, on meeting their needs, and they will be yours. They will follow you.*

This is the first basic principle of what we call charisma.

When we see it at work, when we are on the receiving end of a message aimed at us, tailored to our needs, we are captured by that message. The speaker has drawn our attention, moved us to action or emotion. That, we think, is a powerful speaker. That, we think, is charisma.

Actually, it's simply a speaker who cares more about communicating than she or he cares about being the star.

You don't have to be a professional speaker to make it work, either. I'll let one of our ESI graduates tell you about his experience.

William Bradley Jr. recalls a tuned out audience he turned around using the tools he learned from us. During the year 2000, he served as Vice President of the North Carolina Jaycees. He was speaking to chapters all across the state and was scheduled to deliver a keynote address to one of the largest chapters in the state.

Shortly before he was to go on, he learned that a local charity had been accidentally booked to make a presentation at the same meeting. William graciously agreed to deliver the closing comments instead of the keynote address, and began making mental notes to shorten his presentation.

William recalls that the charity representative was passionate about his subject, but the material was pretty dry. That was followed by a number of Jaycee announcements from a number of members.

"As the meeting wore on, I could feel the mood of the room grow restless," William says. "The hum of casual conversations started to drown out whoever was at the podium. The bar at the far end of the room was becoming a gathering place for the uninterested.

"My mouth went dry knowing I was soon to be the only thing in the way of adjourning the meeting."

Finally, it was William's turn. And, boy, did he inherit a tuned out audience.

"Instead of my usual version of my speech, I wove the members of the Raleigh Jaycees into my story," William says. "I used examples given during the meeting to emphasize my points..."

People's names, local activities became a part of William's message.

"Soon, not a sound could be heard and all 300 pairs of eyes were directed at me. Wow, I had 'em!"

William sent them off with a bang and stepped down to a huge ovation. Quite a turnaround for a tuned out audience. And he did it by using the very simple tools we're talking about in this chapter.

I can't, of course, become Hispanic or a coal miner or a female accountant. And if I try, they'll all know I'm a phony and I still won't to be very effective in my communication.

But if I learn enough about the culture of those Hispanic business owners, those coal miners, those female accountants to understand where they are coming from, I may be able to get their ear. If I show them I have a bit of understanding or

Tuned Out

Try this if you doubt that a tuned out audience can affect your ability to communicate effectively.

Grab a partner and ask him or her to stand face to face, about cocktail-party-distance away, while you talk. Your partner's only function is to avoid eye contact with you at all costs. Ask her or him to look over your shoulder, at the others in the room, at the clock, their watch, a fly on the ceiling.

Now talk to that person for two minutes. See how you react. Can you remain focused on your message? Can you muster enthusiasm for your monologue?

And can your listener tell you much about what you said once it's over?

Connecting with the audience is vital. But you've got the tools to do it.

respect for their beliefs, their environment, their day-to-day existence, I may just convince them that something I have to say is applicable, even beneficial, to them.

If I connect with their world, I open the door for them to connect with mine.

Then we are in dialogue. Then we communicate.

So getting to know my audience and tailoring my message to them is not about selling out. It's about buying into them, so they have the opportunity to buy into my message.

A Conversation with Friends

I always do my homework ahead of time. I always prepare my presentations based on the general information I've put together about my audience.

The next step to connecting with my audience is to show up early.

Arriving early serves many purposes. I get to walk around and meet people. Learn their names, look them in the eye, do a little socializing. I find it helps get the audience on my side, makes them more willing, eager even, to like me and my message.

But here's what's most important: *When I show up and mingle, I find out the audience is made up of people just like me. I find our common ground.*

They're ordinary people with wants and needs, families and sick children, power bills and toothaches. It's comforting to

Audience Signals

Here's what you'll see when the audience is with you:

» They're leaning forward.

» There's a hush in the room.

» They return your eye contact.

» They react quickly to your suggestions (laugh more quickly, get out their notebooks more quickly).

Here's what you'll see when the audience is no longer with you:

» They move around, either in their seats or in and out of their seats.

» They make a lot of trips to the coffeepot or the rest room.

» They whisper to one another.

» They rustle papers.

» They don't make eye contact.

» They doze off.

know that I'm speaking to individuals I've already met and befriended to some extent, rather than to some nameless, faceless, unknown quotient.

Then, when I'm presenting, I can interact with the audience just the way I would interact if I were having a conversation over dinner with friends. I can relate little stories or observations I've gotten just prior to standing up to speak. I can call people by name. And nothing connects an audience with you more than speaking to Sam or Leigh or Tracy or Mike.

By showing up early, I also have the opportunity to fine-tune my knowledge of what this audience wants and needs from me. Then I can do some last-minute adapting of my material—as William Bradley did with the Raleigh Jaycees.

I realize that in some circumstances this is more difficult. At some national conferences, for example, several sessions are often going on at once, resulting in audiences who move around, come and go. But I don't have to make a personal connection with each individual in the audience in order to know the lingo, the personality, the passions of the group. I can still speak to a few of the individuals in the room, or about something that happened the night before at the opening session or the awards banquet we'll all be attending that evening. The process still works.

The end result of all this is that we are speaking to individuals in an intimate conversation. We're chatting with friends as opposed to making a staid presentation to a group of strangers. Instead of stiff and scary, the situation suddenly becomes fun and comfortable.

Making a Difference in Someone's Life

What I'm doing, I realize, is asking you to make a profound change in the way you view yourself and your role as a communicator. It's a change some of us—especially those of us who bring a lot of innate skill to the task—resist.

After all, those of us who enjoy our role as presenter—as actor—didn't get into it because we're the shy and retiring type.

We didn't always get into it to help somebody else; we most often got into it because we loved the attention, the adulation.

I liked being center ring. I liked the applause.

Then I began to see myself more clearly in disastrous interviews like the one with Jonathan Winter; and in successful dialogues like the one with Clint Eastwood. I made the circuit in the late '70s and early '80s with some of the biggest guns in motivational speaking—Dr. Norman Vincent Peale, Paul Harvey, Zig Ziglar, Dennis Waitley, Cavett Robert, Art Linkletter—at enormous rallies at places like San Francisco's Cow Palace. It became evident to me that I was more effective introducing those great speakers if I condensed the introduction into the wants and needs of the audience, focusing on the audience and the people I was introducing. With me, and my ego, totally on the outside.

The less I focused on me and the more I focused on others, the more effective I was.

In 1980, a couple of guys—Tom Carpenter with Aetna Life Insurance and Rick Dyer with Apple Computer—asked me to train their people to become more effective communicators. That training session became the most profound learning experience I'd ever had. It was my trial by fire, to learn to coach instead of taking center stage. I learned the powerful gift of making a positive difference in someone's life.

And that is only possible through effective communication. And effective communication requires dialogue.

Of course, engaging in dialogue also implies that I do something besides speak. It implies that I **listen**. Believe it or not, some of us are less effective at listening than we are at speaking. But we can learn.

Quick Connections

If you're looking for a few simple but effective ways to instantly connect with an audience, even a tough audience, try these.

ASK A COUPLE OF MEANINGFUL QUESTIONS. Don't make them difficult questions, of course. Questions literally get you into an active dialogue with your audience, even if you're simply asking a yes or no question that requires nothing more than raised hands or nods.

Even more effective in some situations are questions that require real answers from the audience. For example, at ESI we always begin by asking attendees what common traits they see in effective speakers. We begin a list on a blackboard or flip chart. This loosens people up every time. It gives us information about our audience, and begins to acquaint us with their personalities, too.

KNOW WHAT YOU WANT. Look at your audience, see them, realize they're real people and decide what you want from them. Do you want to surprise them, stir them, interest them, inspire them, make them change, amuse them, make a friend of them? Define your goal then go after it.

USE FACTS AND FEELINGS. Individuals respond differently, learn differently and it is our job as communicators to meet them where they are. To communicate in a variety of ways.

One of the broadest differences in our audience members is between those who learn from facts and those who learn from feelings. You can reach them both.

For example, when we want to impress upon ESI attendees the importance of passion for our subject, Ty often refers to a Bowling Green University study of teaching effectiveness, using statistics to illustrate that a higher percentage of students — 90 percent, in fact — prefer teachers with passion over teachers who only know the facts. Then he illustrates that by talking about the high school biology teacher who put him to sleep every day with her facts, contrasted with his fascination for the PBS programs hosted by Carl Sagan. Both covered the same topics. Only one set him on fire.

It's the same information, but delivered using a different method. Everybody in the room connects with either the statistics or the storytelling, the facts or the feelings. Use both and you'll discover you connect with everyone in the audience.

LOOK THEM IN THE EYE. Chapter Six includes information on effective eye contact. Read it, learn it, use it. Don't be afraid to look them in the eye.

BE VULNERABLE. Do you remember the earlier discussion about the power of being vulnerable? We must learn to be private in public, to be open and trusting instead of guarded.

That doesn't mean telling all about your escapades. It might mean demonstrating one of your points by telling the story of a time when you missed the boat entirely. It might even be as simple as pausing at powerful moments, allowing your emotions to show. It is the willingness not to be perfect. To laugh at yourself. To enjoy the moment.

But remember this: It never means telling them you're afraid or unprepared. That makes them nervous. So keep that one to yourself.

Ch. 5 CHARISMA, PART TWO : LISTEN UP!

« This book is not about how to speak. This book is about how to communicate. »

Calvin Coolidge, famous for being tight-lipped, put it this way: Nobody ever listened themselves out of a job.

What he was trying to say, of course, is that anytime we open our mouths there is the potential for getting ourselves in trouble. For miscommunicating. For inserting our foot.

I've done it. Bet you have, too.

But there is the other side to communication. The side of communication that turns monologue into dialogue. The side of communication that adds to the aura of charisma for anyone who uses it. The side of communication that gets far too little attention.

Listening.

I'll tell you how critical listening skills are. I've never encountered a book on building a better marriage, or a therapist who specializes in healing troubled marriages, that doesn't emphasize learning to listen effectively. In fact, one such book I recall asserts that it's downright criminal that we don't teach listening skills in every school in this country.

That's hard to argue with. It's also hard to argue with your mother, and mine used to tell me there was a reason God gave us two ears and only one mouth: So we would talk only half as much as we listen.

Unfortunately, we sometimes decide we know so much that the world may tip on its axis if we don't share what we know. So we talk. And talk. And talk.

I was with a friend just this morning and was finally able to put my finger on the reason we're not better friends. I can't finish a sentence without being interrupted because this person is constantly being reminded of something so critical it must be said at that very moment. There's a good lesson for me in that. As I move forward on my own journey to better communication, I begin to recognize the huge reward in asking myself whether this is a moment when I can simply keep quiet.

I am learning to be an effective *communicator*, not simply an effective *talker*.

So let me remind all of us, once again, that this book is not about how to **speak**. This book is about how to **communicate**. How to do more than monologue. How to dialogue.

It was an epiphany for me early in my broadcasting career to learn that listening made me more effective—more successful, even—than talking. If I had a guest I really respected and wanted to know more about, I tended to ask questions and be very quiet and listen. And those interviews always received the highest ratings. One of my passions is politics and when I had the opportunity to interview people like Richard Nixon, Jimmy Carter or Sam Irvin, I would ask simple questions, then nod and give listening sounds. Tell me more, I was saying. The payoff was always better interviews.

I learned to do the same with movie stars, academics, business giants.

But some of us are so busy talking, or preparing to talk, or thinking about the next lull in the conversation that will permit us to talk, that we don't take the time to listen. We're so concerned with polishing our speaking skills that we overlook the invaluable skill of listening.

Remember, all of us today receive more demands on our time and attention than ever before. We're on information overload. Everybody wants our attention. And who are we most likely to listen to? The person who's paying attention to us, to our needs, to our concerns, to our interests.

We'll listen to the people who listen to us.

A friend of mine recently made a stop at a small card shop. When she entered the store, one of the employees asked if she needed help finding something. My friend said no, and was pleased with the indication that her business mattered to the shopkeeper. Within a few moments, another store employee approached her and asked the same question. And in a few moments, the first store employee asked again.

"By that time," my friend said, "I was so aggravated by the constant barrage that I was ready to walk out of the store. Clearly, they weren't listening to me."

The lesson for us, as service providers, as sales associates, as executives—as communicators—is to learn to listen.

As I say to those I coach, our job as presenters isn't so much to **get the attention** of our audience as it is to **give attention** to our audience.

Active Listening

How do we give attention to an audience? How do those of us with a passion for communicating our message apply the brakes long enough to listen?

First, we must become more attuned to the idea of listening. Stephen R. Covey, who has reached millions with "***The 7 Habits of Highly Effective People***," mentions listening when he suggests that we seek to understand others before we try to get them to understand us. And before him, St. Francis of Assisi wrote a prayer also used by millions, which says, in part, "O, Divine Master, grant that I may not so much seek...to be understood as to understand...for it is in giving that we receive..."

These wise words tell me it's a lot more important for me to understand others than it is for others to understand me. He's also saying that if I make the effort to understand others instead of babbling on about what I want them to understand about me, I will get everything I need. *It is in giving that I receive. In giving attention—in listening—I receive all the attention I need.*

If I listen to them, they will listen to me.

So I must cultivate a listening mindset. I must strive to project myself into the minds of my audience members. I must strive to be the kind of speaker I'd want to listen to, the kind of salesperson I'd want to buy from. I must find out what my customers, my listeners, my audience members are going through, what they are thinking, what they need.

Fortune magazine interviewed Ross Perot years ago about what he would do to turn around General Motors. Now, think what you will of Perot's efforts in the political arena, but he has some terrific insights on listening. In fact, the thread running through the entire interview was listening. Among the things Perot said he would tell top GM officials was, "Starting today, in order to build the finest cars in the world, GM will listen to its customers, listen to its dealers who sell the cars to customers, listen to the men and women who assemble its cars in the factories, and listen to the engineers who design its cars.

"The watchword will be: 'Listen, listen, listen' to the customers and the people who are actually doing the work. Their ideas, fresh from the marketplace, will make GM the best in the world."

All of us must become active listeners.

How do we do that? Using our listening tools is simple, really, once we become convinced and committed. After all, as Mother always said, we come equipped with twice as many listening tools.

Listen to These Tips

Let's look at the tips and techniques for becoming better listeners, what we call active listeners.

»Ask questions.

»Don't interrupt.

»Be flexible.

»Demonstrate that you're listening.

»Listen accurately.

»Listen without distractions.

»Tolerate silences/pauses.

»Withhold judgment.

These eight vital tools enable you to make giant headway in becoming more than a speaker, a presenter, a performer. They move you along the path to becoming a true communicator by involving you actively in the process of listening to others. By opening your ears **and** your eyes, you learn from every signal your audience sends, including words, tone of voice, and body language. If you pay attention, you will hear what they are telling you even if they never open their mouths.

Let's take a closer look at these active listening skills.

Ask questions—and listen to answers. As an active listener, we must be as sensitive to the needs and concerns of our audience members as we are capable of being. We invite their involvement by seeking their input and their opinions, whether they are customers in a one-on-one situation or audience members in a larger venue. Ask for a show of hands. Poll the audience and keep a running list of their responses on a flip chart. Invite their feedback. Then use what they tell you to focus the rest of your presentation.

Asking questions builds trust. And trust opens the door for true communication.

Don't interrupt. One of the clearest signals that we aren't listening is when we jump in to add our two-cents' worth while someone else is talking. And we set the stage for that in our minds, when we're preparing our rebuttals before they've even completed a thought.

Be flexible. Use what you hear from customers, audiences, colleagues, to draw up a new roadmap, if necessary. If a listener tells you what's important, pay attention. Respond. Go down the road that's been pointed out to you.

Most of us tend to listen for what we expect, and we will most often hear what we listen for. So be open, be flexible. Speaking with an agenda is often our purpose, but don't take that to mean that we should also listen with an agenda.

Demonstrate that you're listening. Now that you realize how easy it is to pick up the signals others send, make sure you're sending signals of your own. Maintain eye contact. Nod. Smile. Lean forward. Make non-intrusive comments—"Yes," "Exactly," and so forth—that will not only signal your interest but will encourage the speaker to continue.

My bride and partner, Pat, used to think I was the world's worst listener because I failed to acknowledge what I was hearing. She has taught me to let her know that I value and pay attention to her by saying, "Tell me more" or "Then what?"

African-American churches with their call-and-response style of worship offer a vivid example of true communication between speaker and audience. When the preacher strikes a chord, members of the congregation either individually or collectively respond with a heartfelt "Amen!" Their enthusiasm feeds the passion of the preacher and a cycle of powerful dialogue has been born. The result is electric.

Listen accurately. Research shows that after listening to a ten-minute oral presentation, the average listener has heard, understood, properly evaluated and retained only about half of what was said. Only half! And within forty-eight hours, approximately half of that has been forgotten. In other words, listeners retain only about 25 percent of what they heard two days ago.

We're not using those two ears very effectively, are we?

Pat has probably taught me more about listening well than anyone else in my life. She constantly reminds me that ineffective listening gets us in more trouble than ineffective speaking. And that's as critical, she says, in our personal relationships as it is in our professional ones.

"When you have six children, you learn to listen," Pat says. "If you don't, you're always making mistakes. You're missing connections, you're missing cues to the things that are of great consequence in the lives of your children."

And you'll do the same thing on the job, with friends, in your social interactions.

To improve the accuracy of your listening techniques, try this in your next half-dozen personal or business conversations: Repeat, restate or rephrase what you thought you heard—*and do so without adding your own opinion*. This is vitally important when taking questions or feedback from an audience, even more so when the dialogue is one-on-one. Then, if necessary based on feedback, clarify the original comment. Summarize the entire exchange. And watch for signs that you still don't have it right. Frowns, frustration, a shaking head tell you that somewhere, communication is failing.

Practice Tool

Grab a friend or colleague and check your active listening skills. Ask the person to talk to you about something, anything, for two minutes. Then make an effort to repeat what was said to you. Begin by saying, "Here is what I heard..." and end with, "Is that what you said?"

Then keep the exercise going until your friend tells you that you got it right.

Afterward, ask your friend for additional feedback. Did you:

- Give physical clues that you were listening? A nod, eye contact.

- Indicate in any nonverbal way that you disagreed with what was being said?

- Repeat their message back to them without adding your own opinion?

- Act distracted at any time?

By the way, one of the best tips for improving the accuracy of our listening is to...

Listen without distractions. A habit we often prize in today's hectic life and business arena is one that gets in the way of effective listening. We're champion multi-taskers. We can talk on the phone and check our e-mail at the same time. We can shop for groceries and answer a page.

When we do that, we are cutting down on the effectiveness of our listening. And we are also signaling others that we aren't giving our full attention to their message. That their message isn't important enough to warrant our undivided attention.

One of our ESI grads, a human resources professional with her company, spoke with pride of her open-door policy at work. Employees were welcome at any time. She had learned to manage the intrusions by continuing whatever work she was already involved in. And when she heard our discussion of listening at ESI, she reports being horrified at the message she was sending to employees: Their problems and concerns did not merit her full attention.

Today, she views herself as a reformed multi-tasker.

So stay in the moment, stay focused on the person or people who are communicating with you.

Tolerate silences. We sometimes call this timing. The effective pause, the moment of emphasis, the fraction of a second that gives the audience time to catch on, to reflect, to react. Timing may not be everything, as some have said, but it is important.

The best use of silence goes beyond mere timing, however. *Silence is best used as a tool for giving others the time, the space, the encouragement to open up.*

Journalists everywhere will tell you that the simplest way to encourage someone to open up, to tell you more, to say the things they might be hesitant to say is to leave them with empty space to fill. Wait for them to speak. Don't fill the

The Payoffs of Good Listening	
We learn more	We retain more information
Others listen to us more	We encourage others to open up
We build trust	Others will be more interested in us

silence yourself. If you can wait out the silences, you will often get straight to the core of what needs to be said, of what you need to hear. This works one-on-one and equally well in front of an audience. If you want them to respond, wait. Don't rush to fill the silence. Wait and listen.

Withhold judgment. Often the only reason we listen to others is to formulate the best way to refute what they're saying.

A good listener is paying attention to what is said not for the purpose of refuting it, but for the kernel of an idea that will enhance understanding for the speaker, the audience. A good listener is striving to understand, not to judge. Because a good listener understands that someone with differing views always has something to teach us. We all learn from the opposing viewpoints, the objections, the disagreement of others—as long as we maintain an open mind.

Listening critically rather than openly creates roadblocks to true communication and understanding. Being a good listener suggests that we be willing to entertain and possibly even accept the other speaker's point of view.

So don't just welcome objections—seek them out. Ask for them. Find out where others disagree with you and engage them in dialogue. If you are open to their differing viewpoints, they are more likely to be open to yours.

Never forget this: If you are judging instead of listening with an open mind, your body language will betray you. Something in your stance, your face, your gestures, your expression will tell the person you're trying to communicate with that you've judged and found him lacking.

What do you think that will do to the trust you're trying to build? The communication you're hoping to foster?

Expanding Your Toolbox

A friend who is a member of a Twelve-Step recovery program tells us this is a part of the incredible power of recovery meetings. It is sometimes the first place an individual has been where others truly listen. When a Twelve-Stepper speaks at a meeting, there are no interruptions, no distractions and no judgment.

No matter how good a listener you are today, there is always room to improve, to grow. Make a commitment today to expand that part of your toolbox. It will enhance every part of your life.

Personally, as I have learned to listen more and better, I have discovered greater enjoyment in all my interactions and greater rewards in meeting my own objectives.

Finally, remember this: If you are a good listener, you will always be perceived as an interesting person. Simply by being **interested**, you will be judged **interesting**.

Are You Listening?

coach speaks

We'd all like to think we're good listeners. But the painful reality is that those of us who need to improve our listening skills are also the ones least likely to hear the signals that we're falling short.

Here's what to listen for, the signals from our loved ones and colleagues and companions that indicate we aren't listening as effectively as we could be.

» How often does someone tell you, "That isn't what I said"?

» How often do you catch yourself in a conversation preparing your next comment instead of focusing on what is being said to you?

» Do you ever forget information almost as soon as you've heard it—someone's name, hometown, occupation.

» Do you often find that everyone else knew the details of a plan, an event, an activity—everyone except you? And, upon further checking, someone says, "I told you that last week."

» Do you sometimes discover that everyone else recalls an event or conversation differently than you? Or more vividly than you?

» Are you guilty of multi-tasking? How often?

Any of these can be signs that your listening skills could stand improvement.

FIRE YOUR BODYGUARD

« A deadpan message is not going to move anyone to action, to emotion, to change. »

Ask yourself this: How comfortable would you feel the next time you take your car in to track down that annoying little ping if the mechanic had nothing but a screwdriver in his toolbox?

Or suppose you've got a leaky faucet and the plumber shows up with only a socket wrench in her tool belt. Suppose you'd feel a little uneasy? A little concerned the job might not get done right?

Pat, my business and life partner, says if all you've got is a hammer, all your problems look like nails.

You've got a toolbox. It's full—chockfull of priceless communications tools. But if you're like most presenters, you're only using a couple of your tools. You're slamming the lid shut, keeping the rest of your tools under wraps. And like most presenters, you'll probably put up a pretty good fight when I ask you to take a few of those rusty tools out and put them to work.

Using them, you'll say, is "just not me." Or, "But I feel phony."

But you're letting such **potent** tools go to waste. Gestures. Posture. Eyes. A face that's expressive, enlivened, not blank or frozen in seriousness. Purposeful movement. Vocal variety.

Your words alone will not do the job. A deadpan message is not going to move anyone to action, to emotion, to change.

Listen to me! You've got a million-dollar toolbox in your hands. Don't slam it shut!

I know what you'll say. I know because I hear it every time we open the doors at the Excellence in Speaking Institute.

"Well, Ty, that's fine for you. But it's just not me. I'm kind of low-key. I've always been serious. Business-like. This is who I am and I'm not comfortable trying to be something I'm not."

Heard it all before. You're not unique.

Guess what? You're not as effective as you can be, either.

And, by the way, it **is** you—the you that you're holding back, stifling by being on guard against feeling foolish or becoming vulnerable. It's almost as if you mentally employ a bodyguard to keep you stiff, formal, safe from expressing the enthusiasm and energy we all naturally feel before we learn to rein ourselves in.

Please...for the moment, suspend judgment. I'm not going to ask you to fire the bodyguard that's keeping your physical tools under lock and key. But sending him out for coffee wouldn't be a bad idea. And while he's gone, let's explore your valuable assets.

Let's jump out of the box we place ourselves in. Let's stop worrying about our level of comfort. Communication isn't about how comfortable we are. It's about how comfortable the **listener** is and how **effective** the sender is.

Look at it this way. If you've got a teenaged son or daughter, or niece or nephew, you wouldn't say, "Okay, you're eighteen now. You're cooked. Done. No need to do any growing, any changing. Right this minute you're everything you'll ever need to be in life."

Of course we wouldn't. Because we know better. We know that teenager is going to make leaps of progress over the next twenty years of her life. She's going to gain wisdom, learn to dress differently, add to her mental and emotional portfolio in ways she never dreams the day she picks up her high school diploma.

If we're lucky, we learn all our lives. Lifetime learners. Students forever.

So get lucky. Let's learn.

The Actor's Tools

Often in business we're taught that it's wise not to show our hand. Negotiators play it close to the vest, we're told. Keep a poker face.

But we're not negotiating here, we're *communicating*. So let's not hide the tools.

Lou Solomon, one of our ESI instructors, sees that business-reserve mindset all the time.

"People have laid down the tools of communication in the name of being professional," Lou says. "We think we shouldn't risk anything when we stand up to speak, that a lifeless face, a monotonous tone is somehow more business-like. The idea of getting animated, being expressive, using gestures doesn't fit our idea of the serious corporate pose.

"But that idea interferes with authentic expression."

The tools we're talking about right now are the performer's tools. But don't take that the wrong way. Actually, we are performing all the time, with family, business associates, lovers. I differentiate between "performing" and "acting," which is trying to convince others you are someone you aren't. And if you'll think about Lou's final comment, "performing" is about conveying authentic expression, the deepest, truest you.

So one aspect of becoming an effective communicator is to become an effective performer. We use these tools to show who we are, and to infect the listener with our enthusiasm.

A look at the most powerful messages—and messengers—proves that the power is not in the words alone. The power is in the presentation, as well. Consider JFK, when he issued his memorable challenge to the American people: *"Ask not what your country can do for you. Ask what you can do for your country."* The words are certainly powerful, but I ask you to consider whether those words would still resonate more than 40 years later if Kennedy had not understood the power of a pause, the power of leaning forward to convey urgency, the power of direct eye contact.

With the right use of the right tools, a good speech becomes great.

We're going to discuss four vital tools, at least a few of which I'd wager you keep stashed in your toolbox, under the watchful eye of that bodyguard you employ.

Face. Eyes. Physical presence, which includes balance, movement and gestures. Vocal variety.

Let's take them out of the box one at a time. Let's talk about how to use them, and how using them will result in almost instant pay-off.

Face: Anne Boyd Gellman is one of the best image consultants I know, as well as an ESI instructor. And that assessment has nothing to do with the fact that she's one of my immensely talented and charming daughters. When Anne coaches, she's often heard to say, "If you're happy, let your face show it."

Deadpan is deadly. Use your face. Let your face convey whatever message your words would convey. Show surprise, disappointment, disbelief, horror, sorrow. And, yes, delight. Smile. A smile of compassion, of empathy, of humor, of connectedness.

Smiles are power. There is nothing weak or lightweight in a smile.

Cam Marsten, another of our instructors who is also a top presenter on how to communicate with Gen Xers, points up the importance of "face" in effective communication in this story about a presentation to the local Bar Association. He and Lou Solomon were talking on presentation skills, which we all know is a vital skill for an attorney.

"We thought we were bombing in a big way," Cam says. "Everything we said was met with dead stares. No smiles, no laughter, no encouraging nods. Lou and I were wondering where the back door was, and how quickly could we beat it out of there.

"Later, we got a letter from someone in attendance telling us how much they got out of our presentation, how much they enjoyed it."

That group of attorneys was using the dead stare they employ to keep others off-center during negotiations, or cross-examinations. They had shut down their facial expressions. And the interesting thing is that the tactic short-circuited effective communication from the audience back to the presenters.

Here's another example from a recent ESI grad, Alan Reed with Reed's Dairy in Idaho Falls. When Alan first came to us, he guarded his professionalism to the point of being downright stiff. With a little gentle persuasion, we discovered that Alan had a quick wit and a real warmth for people. But he was managing to hide it very well in his communication with others.

Alan tells us one of his problems as owner and operator of a family dairy was communicating with employees who needed to improve their work in certain areas. He talked to them, but they never seemed to make a change.

"They would leave my office and still do the same things they had been doing," Alan says.

Clearly, there was a breakdown somewhere in the lines of communication.

"After learning to have more 'face,' as Ty says, to smile more, and to take my responsibilities seriously, but not myself, things have really changed," Alan says. "I can give direction and people listen. They don't take offense to the guidance and really respond.

"I know it's because of my new delivery. People tell me I am more friendly and caring. It's wonderful."

So follow Alan's lead. Allow your face to light up. Allow it to reflect what you're thinking and feeling. It will open the doors to effective communication, even under difficult circumstances.

Eye contact: Pat and I were privileged to take a VIP tour of the White House in the mid '90s. The highlight of the tour, of course, is always the meeting with the President. Now, President Clinton was particularly busy on this visit and there was some possibility he wouldn't drop in on our tour.

But as the tour was about to end, here he came.

Bill Clinton's charisma is, of course, legendary. And on that day, I saw exactly what is behind it.

The tour was a large one, maybe 40 people. And the President's time was very limited. He spent roughly 20 minutes with our group. But as he circulated through the room, he spent a few seconds shaking the hand and *making personal, friendly eye contact* with each person in the room. For only a matter of seconds, he effectively conveyed to each person in that room, "You are the sole focus of my attention. You are important."

As he finished the briefer-than-brief meetings and left the room, my instinctive feeling was, "He liked me best."

And I would stake my retirement account on the fact that every person in the room felt the same way.

All he did was look us in the eyes. For mere seconds. But for those seconds, President Clinton might just as well have been alone in the room with each person. The contact was warm and powerful.

Eye Contact Pitfalls

Eye contact is a powerful tool. And when it isn't used effectively, it can also create a powerful problem. Here are some of the main drawbacks and pitfalls of inappropriate eye contact.

MULTI-TASKING: One of the toughest aspects of using effective eye contact is learning to think and look at people at the same time. One graduate of ESI says, "This is a real problem for me in one-on-one, off-the-cuff conversation. If I'm looking into your eyes, I find it hard to keep my thoughts focused. So I look over your shoulder. And I can tell it's disconcerting to people. I've watched people turn, look around to see what I'm looking at. So I know my effort not to get distracted is distracting to them." A key to success here is to become so comfortable with your material that you can keep your focus no matter what the distraction. We'll discuss that in Chapter Ten.

THE STARE: Learn to recognize the fine line that separates the intense gaze from the overpowering stare. It's partly a matter of timing—several seconds in a group setting is plenty to make the connection. And it's also a matter of facial expression. A lengthy, stone-faced stare gets uncomfortable very quickly. Put a smile on that same face and the entire tone of the exchange shifts.

NARROW FOCUS: When we first begin beefing up our eye contact, some of us have the tendency to direct too much eye contact at one or two people in the audience. Sometimes, at someone you like the most or feel the most comfortable with, or at the person who is acting the most interested. Or, and this one can be fatal in a number of ways, at the boss or decision maker. That can be a turn-off both to the one receiving the eye contact and to the others in the audience who perceive that you don't value their attention and presence.

Work on moving your eye contact around the entire room at regular intervals throughout your presentation. And work on letting your gaze land on someone different each time.

GLARING BACK: Of course, one reason we avoid eye contact is because we're afraid of what we'll see out there. We're afraid of coming across the guy who's nodding off, communicating to us very clearly that we're not exactly enthralling everyone. Or, worse yet, we're afraid of landing on an intimidating face. A hostile face.

In my experience, that happens very rarely. Most people in our audience are predisposed to like us and our message. But it does happen. We'll talk about how to handle a hostile audience member in Chapter Eleven.

I watched, as most of us did, the year 2000 presidential candidates as they swept through crowds, shaking hands, smiling, trying to charm their way into the White House. I was struck by the contrast in the way Al Gore conducted those friendly mob scenes and the way his predecessor conducted them.

If you watch Bill Clinton closely in such a situation, he is doing precisely what he did during that VIP Tour of the White House. He isn't just shaking hands, he is making eye contact with as many of those people as he can. For fifteen seconds, he is the best friend of whomever he's looking at.

When he does that, the intensity of his gaze comes across **even** to the television audience.

In similar circumstances, Al Gore was also working the crowd, making his way through the crush of people, shaking hands, smiling. But, especially early in the race, his eyes were skating over the tops of their heads. He was not making eye contact with many. The impact of that was profound. His smile came across as less than genuine, because it didn't reach his eyes. He connected with few, and therefore was seriously hampered in engaging their emotions.

And, astonishingly enough, the difference was apparent even when I viewed it on television. I'll bet even viewers who aren't attuned to presentation skills felt the distance Gore created.

Don't you wonder how different the outcome of that election might have been if Al Gore had been more skilled at connecting? The race was so close; perhaps it was the difference between making eye contact and not quite making eye contact.

Karen Kinnison, an assistant vice president with Bank of America, tells us that looking people in the eye has been her greatest transformation as a communicator since attending ESI.

"Before...I would talk to the air or around a person's face or look away when speaking or dart my eyes shyly away from theirs, especially when talking to a man," Karen says. "The result of changing this practice is more personal respect and more effective relationships.

"I've found that if you don't look into others' eyes and allow them to look into yours, your message and presence are somewhat 'soulless'."

That is powerful transformation.

You can create that impression of eye contact even in a very large audience, perhaps with lighting that isn't conducive to real eye contact. Sweep a section of the audience slowly, pausing before moving on. And just as was the case with President Clinton, even those in a large audience will feel the visual connection you make with one or two.

I realize that what I'm suggesting isn't comfortable for everyone, as Karen Kinnison indicates. But those I've coached who are shy or otherwise reluctant to make direct eye contact have learned that doing the thing they fear—and acting as if it comes naturally—is ultimately the key to overcoming the fear, the shyness. Do the thing you fear and you master it, rather than allowing it to master you.

We'll talk more about that in Chapter Twelve.

It's important to add here that eye contact sometimes has different connotations in different cultures. We were in Australia recently, working with people from all over the Pacific Rim. One man spoke with his head down out of respect for his audience. In the Japanese culture, only those of equal status share eye contact. And in China, eye contact is sometimes confrontational. So if you do business outside the US, know the cultural implications of eye contact.

But in our culture, eye contact is a powerful tool.

Use your eyes as ambassadors of good will. Connect with people as if you were having a one-to-one conversation. When you do, this visual rapport will relax you and reinforce your sense of confidence.

Eye contact creates intimacy and connectedness. It is the highway on which communications travel.

Physical presence: When you stand in front of an audience, the individuals in that audience evaluate you immediately. Yes, they're looking at your clothes, your hair, the expression on your face—all those things contribute to the image you create.

But the way you stand and position yourself also speaks volumes. Posture and balance communicate something vital about what you think of yourself. And your audience will not afford you any more respect than you give yourself.

Do you slouch? Do you lean? Do you shove your hands in your pockets or cross your arms tightly across your chest, drawing yourself into the smallest target you can create?

Or do you stand tall? Is your body open to your audience? Do you carry yourself in a way that exudes friendly, approachable confidence?

Daughter Anne, in her image consulting, spends much of her time instilling awareness of poise and posture, particularly in her female clients. "Even women who are smaller in stature can create a powerful presence in the way they carry themselves," Anne says.

She also points out that the way we carry ourselves has a powerful impact on how we feel, on the kind of emotional energy we bring to our circumstances. "When I'm having a rotten day, I know that if I stand tall and put a smile on my face, I **feel** better. I have more confidence. I might be in some discomfort about what's going on in my life, but when I put that kind of tool to work in my life, when I choose confidence and positiveness, those things begin to manifest in me. I begin to feel better.

"Just smile and stand taller and see how you feel."

She's right.

Pat likes to stress that other aspects of our physical presence also affect not only the way others see us, but the way we see ourselves, and therefore the way we conduct ourselves. In a world where Dress Down Friday has crept into the rest of the week, for example, casual attitudes are more prevalent in all areas of life and business. With results we didn't expect.

When coaching others, Pat suggests that the way we dress not only demonstrates how we view ourselves, it becomes a way of either respecting or disrespecting our audience. Her beliefs in this area were formed years ago when she was volunteering in our kids' high school cafeteria.

"The sound of the kids headed for the cafeteria was always like a stampede thundering in your direction," Pat recalls. "But one day, we realized they had arrived almost without our noticing it. They walked quietly, weren't being rowdy or yelling across the hall to their friends."

Pat looked out to see what had made such an enormous difference in this herd of teens.

"It was an Aha! moment for me when I saw how they were dressed," Pat says. "It was class picture day and everyone was dressed up—dress shirts, neckties, dresses, heels. They changed their clothes and changed their actions, their attitudes, their carriage."

Of course, we're all in different arenas. A three-piece suit might not be appropriate in a gathering of landscapers at a hands-on workshop. Or an artsy style might create more connection or even respect if you are a writer or an artist. But know your audience well enough to know you aren't dressing outside the parameters of acceptability.

Two other aspects of our physical presence are so vital I'm going to talk about them separately. One is movement and the other is gestures.

Movement: As vigorously as we urge people to get out of whatever box they've placed themselves in, one of Pat's most memorable coaching successes involved putting a man into a box.

"Sonny was all over the place," Pat recalls. "He paced constantly. We all were exhausted just watching him. And no amount of coaching and feedback were touching his tendency to wander."

So Pat scouted around and found a cardboard box. When it came time for Sonny, a Canadian businessman, to make his next presentation, Pat placed the cardboard box in front of the room and made him stand in it.

"Now use all that energy to tell us something you care about," Pat told him.

And he did.

Not comfortably, maybe. Not perfectly, certainly. But better each time Sonny practiced.

We still use our "Sonny box" for our students whose style is to wander.

And that's the key to all of this. Changing our behavior may not feel comfortable the first time—the first dozen times, even—that we do it. But if we practice, the new behavior becomes ours. If we practice, we soon become as comfortable in our new behavior as we have been in our old.

Unlike our Canadian friend, some of us don't move enough. We cling to a lectern as if it were the only thing keeping us upright. Others of us move way too much. We move purposelessly, working off our nervous energy. Pacing back and forth makes us feel good, but does nothing for our audience.

We have to learn to make our movements work **for** us instead of **against** us.

Fig Leaves and Flashers

We rob ourselves of physical presence with two very simple—and very common-place—stances. One is the Fig Leaf, the other the Flashing Fig Leaf.

THE FIG LEAF: You're standing relatively straight, with your hands clasped in front of you. It's stiff, it has no power, it drops and rounds your shoulders. We sometimes use it to still our hands when we're prone to a lot of nervous gesturing. A better alternative is the Reverse Fig Leaf—hands clasped behind us or—even better—to master a few purposeful gestures and funnel our nervous energy into using them well.

THE FLASHING FIG LEAF: We've got those hands clasped tightly in the classic Fig Leaf. But we're determined to open our toolbox and use some gestures, so occasionally we spread our hands. Then, like a nervous cat who's ventured out from under the sofa and darts back at the first noise, we quickly clasp hands once again. This also looks stiff, does nothing to convey spontaneity or enthusiasm. In fact, it probably calls attention to our stiffness—our nervousness—more surely than the Fig Leaf alone.

fig leaf   the flash   return to fig leaf

One of the first things we must learn is that we won't always have a lectern to hide behind. And it is actually a barrier to effective communication. So we must learn to feel comfortable without the lectern as a prop or a crutch.

Here are some quick tips.

- *Always look like you've got somewhere to go and something to say. Move with purpose. When there's no reason to move, stand planted.*

- *Speak from a balanced position. That means not leaning against a lectern, not draped over a flip chart.*

- *Keep your hinges greased by searching out those good reasons to move: to point at someone who has a question, to move in the direction of that person, to reach for a legitimate prop or visual aid.*

Which brings us to our hands.

Gestures: Here's a good rule of thumb: *If your hands are comfortable, your audience is comfortable.* Pulling fingers, jingling coins in your pockets, the Flashing Fig Leaf, all reveal your insecurity.

Using your hands from a position of power—with authority, with confidence, with ease—lends you power. And those gestures may also lend color and character to your presentation.

One of the most powerful leaders of the twentieth century was Franklin Roosevelt, a man who managed to project strength and confidence from a wheelchair. One of his distinctive gestures was his cigarette holder. He used it as a tool, a punctuation mark for the optimistic message he wanted the American people to hear. That cigarette holder became a part of virtually every caricature and illustration ever done of FDR.

And if you'll notice, the tip of that cigarette holder was always pointed up. Up, like the message he carried.

Here are a few simple tips for using gestures more effectively.

When using visual aids such as a flip chart or chalkboard, always put the chart on the opposite side from your writing hand. This way, you won't have your back squarely to the audience. And remember to use the TTT technique—touch, turn, talk. **Touch** (write or point to) the flip chart, **turn** back to the audience, then **talk** to them. Don't talk while you write. Talk only when you can make eye contact, when your voice won't be muffled as you face the flip chart.

Plan movements as carefully as you plan the content of your talk, and practice them until your gestures, too, are second nature. Watch other presenters and make note of the variety of movements and gestures they use. Then give some thought to how those gestures can punctuate the key points you want to emphasize in your talk; the emotions you want to enhance; the responses you want to generate.

Break up the pace and tempo of your movements. Move quickly to show your excitement, slow down to convey thoughtful deliberation. Jab the air. Clench your fists. Sweep the room with an arm to draw them all in.

NOTE: Using the same movements over and over, at the same speed, the same level of intensity, is as boring as no movement. In fact, that kind of monotony of movement becomes distracting, even irritating, very quickly. Your audience becomes conscious of the limited way you move, the repetitive cadence you mark with your gestures. The monotony of your physical statement will capture their attention more easily than your words.

And eventually, you'll drive them crazy.

Still not ready to fire that mental bodyguard who keeps such a watchful eye on your all-business body image? Then let's have one more conversation about your fear of phoniness. In Chapter Seven we'll look at the difference between your feelings and the perceptions of others.

Ch. 7

LOOKING PHONY
VS FEELING PHONY

*« No matter how you **feel**,*
*you rarely **appear** phony. »*

Let's pause for a moment while I read your mind.

We've talked at length about three of the four tools we're going to borrow from the actor's toolbox. Face, eyes and physical presence, which includes balance, movement and gestures. Nothing exotic. Nothing outrageous.

Yet, inevitably someone brings up the most scorching objection of all to using these basic tools.

We don't want to appear phony.

We don't want to look like someone who's putting on an act, someone who isn't genuine, who is a fake.

That is absolutely true. Phoniness isn't going to win a thing for us. Phoniness is a turn-off, a sure-fire way to alienate anyone you might be attempting to communicate with, from one-on-one situations to a packed auditorium.

I wouldn't encourage you to act phony in any way whatso-ever.

But using our eyes, our facial expressions, our bodies to communicate for us is not phony. There is nothing phony about any of the tools stored in your toolbox. How can it be phony to use tools that are already yours, that you already own?

Granted, using the tools may **feel** phony at first. May make us feel counterfeit or contrived. That's always true when we practice a new skill or a new behavior. But you won't **appear** phony. And I'm going to help you prove that to yourself in just a moment.

Before we get to our little exercise, I'd like to tell you what Pat tells everyone she coaches. Every new behavior we learn, she points out, goes through three stages as our internal computer makes adjustments. That's true whether we're learning golf or the tango or conversational French for our trip abroad.

First, we feel awkward and downright phony. (Have you ever tried a French accent? Talk about feeling phony!) And that feeling of awkwardness is no illusion. But if we keep up our practice, we will soon pass through that stage and progress to the mechanical stage. Maybe we don't have to count the steps in the new dance any longer. We're not exactly graceful, but awkward has been replaced by mechanical.

Eventually, Pat says, if we stick with it, our inner computer adjusts and the new behavior that once felt so phony becomes habit.

From phony to mechanical to habit.

And we all know how comfortable habits are.

Here's what I want you to remember. No matter how you **feel**, you rarely **appear** phony.

We may feel phony, but we don't appear phony. And when it comes to creating an impression during communication, that's a significant distinction.

I told you I'd help you prove this point to yourself. Here's how I demonstrate the distinction between our inner feeling and our outer appearance.

Ask a co-worker across the hall or your spouse or your dinner partner to join you. You'll need some help with this. Now, both of you cross your arms. Go ahead. Fold your arms across your chest in whatever manner you typically cross them. Feels right, doesn't it? Feels natural. Take a look at your

The Three Stages of New Habits

Don't forget the three stages we all go through when developing new behavior:

STAGE 1 : Initially, we feel artificial, contrived, phony.

STAGE 2 : With continued practice, the new behavior becomes mechanical. The feelings that we're faking it begin to subside.

STAGE 3 : With enough repetition, the new behavior becomes a habit. And habits are comfortable.

Remember, the phoniness we feel is all on the inside. To the outside world, we look completely genuine.

partner in this demonstration, make sure he or she is participating, too.

Now I want both of you to reverse the way you typically cross your arms.

How does that feel? Uncomfortable? Awkward?

Now sneak another look across the desk or dinner table. Does your friend or co-worker look uncomfortable?

When we do this at ESI, we usually have about a dozen people gathered around a conference table, and we ask everyone to look carefully at one another. We ask if they see anyone who **looks** uncomfortable. Anyone who looks phony.

The answer, of course, is no.

Talk with your co-worker. Same results?

When we change behaviors, we may feel uncomfortable. We may feel so uncomfortable we also feel ungenuine. But we are the only one who perceives our discomfort. From the outside, our new behavior looks completely natural.

The same is true when we begin to smile more, to use our face to convey our thoughts and feelings; when we make eye contact; when we stand tall and move with purpose; when we use bold gestures to accentuate our presentation. We may feel strange, but *we look perfectly natural.*

At ESI, as we progress from day one to day three, as people begin to open their own personal toolboxes, as people begin to use more gestures and more face and eye contact and vocal variety, we'll eventually ask: At what time did this person appear phony during his or her presentation? The answer from others in the class is that they didn't. Ever.

Yet if we ask the presenter how she or he felt, the answer is often very uncomfortable. Sometimes, they'll even say phony.

The perception of the person practicing new behavior is not the same as the perceptions of those in their audience.

So battle the urge to resist new ways of presenting. Think about firing that bodyguard in your mind, the one who is helping you maintain the illusion of professionalism with your stiffness. Be open to using the tools that will help you widen the group of people with whom you can be effective. Be willing to connect everyone to the substance of your message by doing things that entertain as well as inform.

Communicating with your audience is a matter of how well you use the tools. If you are open, warm, vulnerable, if you use effective eye contact, if you face them with poise and power, you will create a wonderful, intimate relationship with an audience of two or two thousand.

Stretching Your Comfort Zone

coach speaks

If using your tools feels uncomfortable, here's a fairly painless way to grow more at ease using more facial expressions, bolder gestures, a balance of stillness and purposeful movement.

When you practice—and Ty will tell you more about the importance of practice in Chapter Ten—don't rehearse just the words. Rehearse your new tools, as well.

But here's the key to stretching your comfort zone: when you practice, **overemphasize** your gestures, movements, expressions and vocal color. Stand in front of the mirror and get really big, really bold. Be as outrageous as you can force yourself to be.

Then, when you're actually in front of a group, the exaggerated rehearsal will pay off in two ways: You'll feel more comfortable using your tools simply because you practiced. And because you practiced in the extreme, more vibrant use of your tools will seem tame by comparison.

VOICE : Put The Orchestra To Work

« Speak conversationally and colorfully. You will make the audience your friend. »

If you're only going to work on two tools, here are the two: eye contact (Chapter Six) and voice.

Let me admit something: I have changed my mind about the significance of voice more than once over the course of my career. When I first started in broadcasting I spent hours, days, weeks working on diction, on the depth of my voice. My first mentor urged me to consider my voice my primary tool. He did it, so I did it. I did it with all the dedication the Boys of Summer devote to spring training. My voice was my pitching arm, and I wanted it finely tuned.

Later, as I realized the importance of connecting with the audience, of listening, of passion for the message, I knocked voice way down on my list of vital tools.

Today, I realize that swing away from voice was simply the shift in priorities necessary to come back to balance. Voice is not the only tool we need. It is one of many, and at this stage in my life I try to remember that a good balance of all my skills makes me most effective. I'm glad I've shifted far enough to once again realize the importance of voice. It is one of our tools that has immediate and continuing impact on the listener.

No, a stunning voice is not necessary to make a stellar performance. Whatever your natural voice, you can learn to use it to advantage. *But you must learn to use it and use it effectively.*

I know this is true because people stop me in public simply because they recognize my voice. I've been 3,000 miles from home, on an airplane, and had other passengers look over their seatbacks after hearing me speak to the flight attendants and say, "I know you!"

Certainly voice is a God-given talent that gives some people an instant advantage. With the right voice, we believe, we can reach for the stars. Without it, some of us also believe, we're perpetually grounded. Why, just look at the greats. Walter Cronkite. James Earl Jones. Jane Pauley. Look at Meryl Streep, whose phenomenal acting career has hinged on what she can do with her amazing voice.

Certainly the right voice can elevate us several notches in effectiveness, in our ability to capture the attention of our audience, whoever that audience is. A friend who is a golf-industry professional recounts numerous times when he used his resonant baritone—which his wife calls "the daddy voice"—in a last-ditch effort to get results. His successes using that natural gift range from keeping a large audience enthralled even when the sound system failed, to retrieving luggage lost for days in London, a success all of us who travel can appreciate.

A commanding, versatile, rich voice is a powerful tool. No question about it.

But each of us can learn to use our voice to advantage. Each of us can learn techniques—breath, projection, enunciation and vocal variety—that can turn any voice, even one perceived as weak or ineffective, into a valuable tool.

Can you think of some examples of people whose voices weren't exactly made in heaven, but who nevertheless became powerful communicators?

How about Barbara Walters? One of the most memorable skits from the early years of Saturday Night Live was comedian Gilda Radner's impersonation of that legendary newswoman. Walters has a lisp, her voice has a certain nasal quality, but that less-than-perfect voice has made her famous—and powerful—because she's made the most of it. She's learned how to use it very effectively in combination with some of the other tools in her toolbox.

Some of the most memorable leading men from Hollywood's golden years didn't have voices that fit the job description. James Cagney, Humphrey Bogart, Gene Kelly, Jimmy Stewart all had less-than-commanding voices. In more recent years, Kevin Costner and John Travolta could be added to that list. Bill Clinton certainly doesn't have the most commanding voice. But they and others like them learned that the trick is not in changing their natural voices. The key is in maximizing the potential of the voice you have.

Playing the Horn You Were Born With

As you consider putting your voice to better use, there are four key areas I want to stress. They are:

- **Breath**
- **Projection**
- **Diction**
- **Vocal variety**

Each is a tool you can learn to use to your advantage, no matter what your vocal range. It's not so much the pitch of the horn that's important, but the way the tune is played.

Certainly people hear our voices and make judgments about them. Dr. Albert Mehrabian, professor emeritus of psychology at UCLA and a pioneer in the field of nonverbal communication, learned through his research that our voices are only 38 percent of our effectiveness in delivering a message. Now, 38 percent is a lot—compared to only 7 percent for the words themselves—but it isn't enough to make or break you. Compare that 38 percent with the 55 percent Dr. Mehrabian attributes to the message our bodies send.

So your voice is important but not the main reason you'll be an effective presenter.

It isn't important to sound like a cello. A tenor sax, a well-played clarinet, a lilting flute can be as beautiful as any instrument you'll hear. The same is true of your voice. Your vocal assets are powerful and they are diverse. They include fluency,

Backstage Warm-Up

We can all learn from the way actors warm up backstage before a show. Try these warm-up techniques to get your orchestra ready before a presentation:

- Make a sound like a siren, moving from the top of your vocal range to the bottom.
- Make a sound like a motorcycle, revving your lips and mouth.
- Massage and stretch the muscles of your face.

pace, energy level, dramatic pauses, articulation, projection, volume and cadence, which is the ebb and flow of your voice's pitch, from high to low.

Whether you're blessed with that deep, rich cello or a fiddle that struggles to stay in tune, you can build on the instrument you were born with. You can do it using breath, projection, diction and vocal variety.

Factors You Control

The important thing to remember about these four contributors to using your voice effectively is that *these are factors you can control.* Here's how.

Breath: Our breathing habits affect our sound enormously. And many of us have never learned to breathe correctly. Let's learn right now.

As children, most of us were taught to take a deep breath by expanding our chest. Wrong, wrong, wrong. We breathe using our diaphragm. And where is the diaphragm located? Below the chest, right above the area we usually think of as our belly.

Let's have a little biology lesson. The diaphragm is a large muscle attached to the lower ribs, actually separating the chest from the abdomen. When you take a deep breath, the diaphragm is designed to move downward, as well as to move the muscles attached to the ribs. Both these actions create more room in our lungs, thus enabling us to breathe more deeply.

So if we aren't moving our diaphragm, we're only using a fraction of our lung capacity.

Well, that's enough biology for me. But I hope you've at least gotten the message that puffing out our chest is only a part of the breathing process.

Try this. Watch a baby lying on its back, breathing naturally, the way we were intended to breathe. Not influenced by misdirection from well-meaning folks. That baby's tummy seems to swell as it breathes in. And it will contract, or flatten out, as the baby breathes out. Watch the rhythm of breathing in, breathing out.

Now try it yourself. Let that diaphragm expand downward, into the tummy area, to make plenty of room in your lungs. Then watch your tummy flatten again (flat is a relative term for most of us) as you empty the lungs and release the breath. For a really dramatic demonstration, try it lying down with this book on your tummy. If this book's not moving, your breathing is too shallow. Work on moving breath into the diaphragm, into the tummy area.

Many of our students have learned that yoga classes are an excellent place for learning the art of effective breathing. Lilias Folan, a popular yoga instructor affiliated for many years with PBS—and herself a powerful presenter—begins many of her sessions by focusing on the breath. (As a side note, yoga is also a wonderful vehicle for learning balance and posture. The Mountain, for example, is a yoga posture that teaches students to ground themselves by standing tall and balancing the weight evenly on both feet.)

Proper use of breath will also help you relax. And it will assist you in improving the next voice tool.

Projection: When you're breathing deeply and not shallowly, your projection automatically improves. In other words, your voice carries better when it comes from deep in your diaphragm rather than from the back of your throat.

Don't mistake projection for loudness, either. You've heard the phrase stage whisper? Even the softest voice can carry to the back of the auditorium when it isn't coming from shallow

An Explosion of Sound

One of the best exercises I know for improving the clarity of our speech was taught to me in the early days of my broadcasting career. We were taught to spit out certain sounds, to create an explosion of sound.

Practice emphasizing these letters the next time you prepare for a presentation:

B as in **boy**	**J** in **judge**
Ch in lur**ch**	**K** in sac**k**
D in nee**d**	**P** in la**p**
G in di**g**	**T** in boo**t**

If you allow these sounds to erupt forth with a little extra force, you'll be sharpening your diction. And adding a little color at the same time.

breathing. And a soft soprano can carry as effectively as a baritone, if the breath is right.

Ask the help of a friend or co-worker in learning to project your voice different distances and in rooms with different acoustics. Once you've become aware of what your voice can do, you'll be able to make adjustments in any situation.

And remember, effective projection will enable you to adjust your volume, which will not only keep you from sounding monotonous to the audience, but will keep your voice fresher, less prone to hoarseness.

Diction: Do you have an accent? Do you tend to speak too fast or too slowly? Are your words crisp and clear, or a little soft around the edges? Are you confident of your pronunciation, your grammar, your articulation? Do you stammer or lisp or stumble around a lot of uhs and ahs when you speak?

I stack all these under the umbrella of diction. All make important contributions to your effectiveness, none are fatal, all can be cured.

First, let me say that major problems with diction can be addressed with the help of a speech pathologist. Progress is usually rapid under the guidance of a professional. And when we remember that we're dealing with a million-dollar toolbox, whatever it takes to develop a pleasant and effective voice is a modest investment.

Let's look at accents. Very few of us can boast perfect diction, the kind of accent-free voice Walter Cronkite, Diane

A Ban on Non-Words

The most effective way to rid your presentations of non-words is to implement a complete ban on non-words. Get rid of non-words in all your speech—in conversation, in voice mail, every time you open your mouth. In that way, you will be very aware of non-words all the time, including the times in which you stand up to present.

Here's a starting point. Ask a friend, family member or colleague to give you a tap on the hand or another signal every time you use non-words in their presence.

Tape yourself for a while in casual conversation and listen to how many non-words you use. Become aware of when you use them and which ones you use. Answer to the coach on your shoulder. Awareness is the vital first step in taking action to change.

Sawyer or Mike Wallace are blessed with. Some of us—I'm one—grew up in the South, so we may hang onto a bit of a drawl or play fast and loose with –ing on the end of a word. Or if we're from the Northeast, perhaps Rs are a challenge. Another group tends to replace the D sound with a T sound. None of that makes us poor speakers. And a touch of accent or dialect can add color or individuality to our presentations— think of Henry Kissinger and Doctor Ruth and their memorable voices.

But if your regional or ethnic accent is so pronounced that it can hamper communication, acknowledge the limitation and seek help. Make a conscious effort to become your own best coach. Try listening to speakers without accent and learn from them. Consistent practice using tongue twisters also improves articulation.

Another limiting habit of diction is the use of non-words. Ah and uh and kind of, like, you know, okay, well. We use them to fill the silence, to give ourselves time to think, because we're nervous.

Toastmasters, a wonderful organization devoted to develop- ing confident presenters, asks someone at each meeting to be the ah-counter. That person literally makes note of the non- words in a talk. Become your own ah-counter. Learn that a pause, a few moments of silence to collect your thoughts, are not only okay, they sometimes pack quite a punch (see Chapter Five).

If you can eliminate non-words, you will be eliminating the "garbage sounds" that diminish your effectiveness as a communicator.

Which brings us to our final, and most powerful, vocal tool.

Vocal variety: Vocal variety is the antithesis of monotony. It is expressiveness versus flatness. It is resisting the urge to do the safe thing, the consistent thing, over and over. Remember, even the most pleasing part of your presentation taken to excess becomes monotonous.

Vocal variety is using different instruments in your orches- tra. Learn the power of a lilting note, a whisper, a pause or a shout. Don't limit yourself to using only the notes, only the instruments you're familiar and comfortable with. Use new notes as well. Use the full orchestra, fiddle to flute.

What we are describing is the ultimate storyteller's skill. Have you ever sat in at the public library when the children's story hour was going on? Listen to the storyteller. She isn't reading the story all in one tone, all at one speed. She's lowering her voice to a whisper, urging the children to lean in and listen more intently. She's bursting forth with sound, shaking them up, surprising them, exciting them. She's slowing down and speeding up. She's changing her voice to fit the story. She is painting a picture by pulling out certain words, expanding key syllables of the word to make the children take note.

You can do this, too, as you plan and practice your presentation, which we'll begin to talk about in the next two chapters. We're going to suggest that you begin by writing out your presentation, and that gives you the opportunity to focus on how you deliver the words you've scripted. What parts of the presentation warrant intent listening? When do you want to surprise 'em, to jolt them out of their seats? Do you want their hearts racing at one point, or to envelope them in an aura of calm at another time? Diagnose a sentence and see what words you can highlight, elongate, emphasize with your voice.

If you want to listen to a master storyteller, listen to Garrison Keiller on public radio. When he invites us to visit Lake Woebegone, I know I certainly can't resist the trip. It's impossible to listen to him without stopping and devoting all my attention to the pictures he's painting. And he does it all with voice. That's all he's got. Voice.

It's enough. It's more than enough.

Those of us who remember the heyday of radio remember all too well what it was like sitting around that wooden box, hanging on every word. They could turn out the lights and blindfold us and still engage us one hundred percent. In fact, if you haven't listened to some of those classic radio programs lately—or ever—do so. Plenty of them are available for purchase today, or on loan from the library. Listen to "The Shadow." Get your hands on "War of the Worlds." And settle down with the more current "Prairie Home Companion." Listen and learn the magic of storytelling.

A final word about monotony. Certainly, it is a lack of vocal color. But we can also become monotonous in our gestures, our energy, in every part of our presentation. We must work to keep the audience a little off balance. Do not become predictable. Because as soon as you become predictable, you'll become boring.

Voicing a Few Warnings

A few final points.

- Use your voice to make each word work for your message. When we use our voice to emphasize, to move, to stir, we must do it with purpose. Using variety and inflection randomly, without keeping the effectiveness of the message as its focal point, we create dissonance in our listeners.

- When you want an audience to listen closely, turn the volume down. That's right, down. Not up. Beating the air with your voice the way you might beat the podium with your fist is only one way to attract attention—and not always the most effective way to compel the audience to pay close attention. Instead, lower your voice and speak more slowly, deliberately. Strange as it may seem, this draws their focus to your message, too.

- Use pauses. Use them to emphasize key points, after rhetorical questions, or when you've lost your way or drawn a blank. Pauses are always better than non-words and other fillers.

- Resist the urge to hyper-correct yourself. As you work on diction, including pronunciation, enunciation and grammar, don't aim for perfection at the risk of a conversational tone. If you become too stylized, if you become hyper-correct, the effect will be stilted and phony. This may have been another of Al Gore's downfalls in the 2000 Presidential election.

Remember to speak conversationally and colorfully. You will make the audience your friend.

Listen to Yourself

coach speaks

Pretend you're in front of an audience of pre-schoolers. Or better yet, round up the neighbor kids, the grandkids, your nieces and nephews and read them a story. Read them a lot of stories. Use everything you've got to get them laughing or clinging to the edge of their seats.

And record the whole thing—not on video, but audio only. You'll learn amazing things about your weaknesses and your strengths as a storyteller.

Using that same tape recorder, read aloud ten or fifteen minutes at a time several times a week. Play it back. Listen carefully. Listen for color, energy, cadence, pace, diction.

In both these exercises, use the coach on your shoulder to pinpoint your strengths as well as the areas in which you can make improvements.

Ch. 9 SWEATING IN ADVANCE

« Practice.
Practice.
Practice. »

Honest Abe, known for one of the most-remembered speeches of all time, was fond of saying he needed two weeks to write a twenty-minute speech, one week for a forty-minute speech, but concluded, "I can give a two-hour rambling talk right now."

And trust Mark Twain to make a point in a way we'll all remember. He said, "It takes three weeks to prepare a good ad-lib speech."

Speaking succinctly, packing power into a few well-chosen words, conveying a significant message with brevity and impact—all that takes preparation. Some of us like to think we can wing it, and we rationalize that belief in a number of ways. After all, don't we know our own opinion? Don't we talk about this subject all the time? Don't we want to sound spontaneous?

Yes, yes, and yes.

Can't we do that best if we're speaking off the cuff?

No, no and no. At least, not very often. Eventually, the person who relies on winging it will crash and burn.

Think of it this way. A sandlot game doesn't require a lot of preparation. It's all in fun and there's no trophy—or raise or promotion—hanging in the balance. But if we want to take our game beyond the sandlot, if we want to head for the majors, take it to the play-offs, we've got to prepare for it.

Let me tell you about a letter we received from a recent ESI graduate. She was interviewing for a promotion within her present company. Like all the candidates, she was asked to prepare a 15-minute presentation on how her skills met the job requirements, why she was the best choice, that kind of thing.

"I very carefully prepared what I wanted to say, and rehearsed it many times, both on my own and in front of others," Jennifer said. "During the interview I was poised and relaxed…and remembered to say all the things I wanted to say."

Here's the feedback she received.

"The interviewers told me that in all their years of interviewing, they had never had anyone be so eloquent and poised without using any notes…The feedback on how well I did presenting myself made me feel very much like a winner."

She is, indeed, a winner. And the perfect example of what sports reporter George Plimpton meant, in an article on preparing for a speech, when he said, "The more you sweat in advance, the less you'll have to sweat once you appear on stage."

Four Stages of Preparation

We've talked plenty about the various tools and tactics that contribute to successful communication. We've talked about voice and physical presence and listening. Purposeful movement. Connection with your audience.

Another critical component is the words we use.

UCLA professor emeritus of psychology Dr. Albert Mehrabian, author and researcher on nonverbal communication, determined that the actual words we use make up only seven percent of effective communication.

But without that significant seven percent, communication falls apart. Without a message—a valuable message, a clear message, a memorable message—your listeners will eventually recognize that your presentation is an empty suit. As my friends in Texas like to say, all hat, no cattle.

You've got a message. Let's make sure you're using the right words to communicate it.

Most of us find preparation tedious. We'd rather rush out on stage armed with our enthusiasm and our charm and wow 'em. But this part of our toolbox is about leaving them with something that will last long after the applause has died. This is beyond performance, beyond inspiration. This is what the listener takes home.

Let's talk about giving our presentations substance. We'll cover four stages of preparation.

- *Have a central idea or purpose.*
- *Know your audience.*
- *Plan a beginning, a middle and an end for your message.*

You're right. I promised four stages of preparation. And we'll have four. But the final stage is so important we're going to save it for Chapter Ten. So for the moment, let's look at the words, and how we get them organized.

Stage One: Purpose

First, have a central idea or purpose. What do you want to say? And why do you want to say it?

Why do you want to say it?

There's a key point we don't want to overlook. What are you hoping to achieve with this presentation? You have convictions about your topic, passion and enthusiasm for the subject. (If you don't, better back up and pick another one.) But what do you **want** from this audience?

Do you want to inform them, to teach them?

Do you want to inspire them to action or stimulate them to thought?

Maybe you're out to persuade them, convince them, win them over. Sell them, if you will, on your idea or product or service.

Or maybe your main purpose is to entertain, amuse or simply interest them in your topic.

Any and all of those are valid reasons for communication. But before you can achieve success at any of them, you must know what you hope to accomplish. You must have a destination before you know which map to follow.

So know your central idea and your purpose. When you do, you are well-armed.

Stage Two: Know Your Audience

Next, know your audience. We've covered this thoroughly

in Chapter Four, so we won't go into detail here. Just remember that knowing your audience, beginning with a strong connection to them and a knowledge of their expectations, going into a presentation aware that your job is to give them something in return for their attention—all these are critical points as you prepare your presentation.

You're there for them, not vice versa.

David McClelland trains both new and old customers, usually college and university faculty and staff. After our coaching sessions, he began taking extra time to discover the "user knowledge level" of the group he would be presenting to next. He learned that a high number of students at one particular school transferred to a nearby four-year institution.

"When an audience member asked why his students should use my company's software over the competition, I was able to let the audience know that many of their students would transfer to XYZ school in the future, where they would also be using my product," David says.

The extra time he'd spent researching his audience had paid off in a solid answer to a potentially tough question from the audience.

If you still need the idea of knowing your audience reinforced, take a few minutes right now to re-read Chapter Four.

Knowing your audience gives you material to work with. It gives you anecdotes they can connect with, details of time and place and circumstance that will establish you as someone who knows and understands where they are coming from.

If you've spoken to someone ahead of time about these people, their jobs, their beliefs and values, you will have valuable information as you prepare your talk. If you've read their professional and trade journals or visited their web sites, you will know their lingo. If you've checked out their local newspaper, you'll have some idea of their environment, their immediate concerns, the flavor of their lives.

All this is material you can put to work in seeing the audience as real human beings, and in demonstrating to them that you do.

Know your message and your purpose. Know your audience.

Stage Three: Plan the Words

Plan a beginning, a middle and an ending for your presentation.

It's time to start selecting the specific words that will convey your message and purpose for this audience. Most folks, especially in the beginning, will want to write down their words because they don't want to leave their effectiveness to chance.

Writing anything strikes many people as an overwhelming task. Getting organized, choosing the right words, paying attention to grammar and spelling, grinding away from one sentence to the next in a way that is logical and informative and interesting. Writing is a big job. And as Abe Lincoln pointed out, boiling down a powerful message into five minutes is actually harder than figuring out how to say it in five hours.

But there are a number of formats that take the headache out of organizing and writing a presentation. We'll look at several of the best ones, explain how they work. Then you can select the one that sounds best to you. Or you can experiment with all of them until you find the one that works best for you. There's no wrong or right in preparing a presentation, as long as you remember the three key elements: the beginning, the middle, the end.

Before we look at organizational formats, let's talk about the first step in organizing anything—fleshing out our idea. Capturing all the most vital information so we can see the information we have to work with.

Brainstorm with yourself, or with others if that's appropriate. On a flip chart or a legal pad, jot down every single idea you can generate that is related to the topic. Verbalizing ideas without editing or otherwise inhibiting their flow, as we all know, generates the flow of additional ideas. Ideas spawn ideas and soon you'll have an entire page of ideas. Then, you can begin to cluster those ideas, connecting points that logically group together. These clusters become the main points around which you organize your presentation.

Once you've brainstormed your idea, it's time to structure those ideas into a coherent and cohesive presentation.

Giving it Structure

One of four simple organizational structures can be used to develop a great presentation. In each of these four formats, we recommend devoting roughly 15 percent of your talk to the introductory material, 75 percent to the body or middle of the presentation, and 10 percent to your conclusions.

Let's look at these four formats:

- *Tell 'em*

- *PREP*

- *SOS*

- *PPF*

Any presentation you make can be successfully and effectively organized under one of these formats.

Tell 'em: I love this one because it couldn't be simpler. First, in your introduction (15 percent, remember), tell the audience what you're going to tell them. For example, if you're talking about leadership skills, you could say, "By the time you leave here today, you'll have at your disposal the three most vital tools a leader needs to inspire team members." Or, "Research has identified the four areas in which most leaders fall short. Today, I'm going to share those shortfalls with you, and tell you how to avoid them yourself."

You've told them what you're going to tell them.

Then, in the body of the talk, that all-important 75 percent that is the meat-and-potatoes of your presentation, you're going to tell them what you promised to tell them. You tell them about those three vital tools, or the four areas in which leaders fail. You're going to support each of those main points with support data.

You've told them what you promised to tell them.

Finally, in that last 10 percent of your talk, you're going to conclude by telling them what you've told them. You'll say, perhaps, "You now know the four ways in which most leaders fail. So you can leave here today equipped to succeed where others fail."

Tell 'em. Tell them what you're going to tell them, tell them, then tell them what you told them. Simple. Effective.

PREP: This acronym stands for **P**oint of view, **R**easons, **E**vidence, **P**oint of view restated. Very similar to the Tell 'em format, PREP suggests that you begin with a statement of your point of view (that introductory 15 percent), give them the reasons and the evidence that support your point of view (75 percent), and conclude with restating your point of view (10 percent).

For example, you could begin with the opinion, "Having a clear vision of where you're going and what you hope to achieve will not guarantee your success. The successful leader must be able to communicate that vision to others. You may have the idea of the century and millions of dollars to back it, but if you lack the ability to inspire others with that vision, you cannot succeed."

A very definite point of view. Now, back that point of view with the reasons you arrived at it, followed by the evidence-- facts, data, anecdotes—that it is true. Lead your audience to the unmistakable conclusion that your original statement is correct. Tell them how to go about sharing their vision with those they would lead. Remember, this makes up 75 percent of your message.

And finally, come back to your point of view and close with a restatement of your point of view: "If you learn how to communicate your vision, you cannot fail to turn that vision into reality."

Point of view, reasons, evidence, point of view repeated.

SOS: **S**ituation, **O**ptions, **S**olution. This is an excellent format for an impromptu presentation. Begin by outlining the situation. "We're here today because it is time to decide whether or not to cut the departmental budget." Then, present options, including the advantages and disadvantages of those options. This is that 75 percent that makes up the body of your presentation. Then conclude with a solution. "Having weighed each of the options, the clear solution is a temporary freeze on new hires."

PPF. Past, **P**resent and **F**uture. I suggest this simple format whenever you're asked to "tell us about yourself" or when you have a new project you hope to sell to the board. Past, or this is how it was (15 percent). Present, this is how it is (75 percent). Future, this is how we hope it will be (10 percent).

For example, "Two years ago, we approached our budget shortfalls with a 'wait-and-see' attitude." After a brief discussion of that decision, you spend the majority of your discussion on the problems created by that past decision. "As a result, today our previous budget shortfalls have become a sea of red ink. Without immediate action, we face..." And conclude with what the future holds. "If we adopt the proposal now on the table, we can be back in the black by this time next year."

Past, present, future.

Grabber Openings

The purpose of your opening is to grab the attention of your audience away from whatever has their attention at that moment. You want to capture their interest right away. And that isn't easy, given the fact that in any given audience someone is thinking about the birthday party for their toddler, or the request for a raise that's just been turned down, or the builder who is two months behind schedule.

Here are some tips for creating grabber openers:

- Ask a thought-provoking question. "What are the chances you'll still be married five years after you say 'I do'?"
- Tell a relevant joke.
- Make a startling statement.
- Use a powerful quotation. Look back at the beginning of this chapter for an example.
- Give a potent example or illustration.
- Point out a significant historic event.
- Compliment the audience.
- Use a visual or auditory gimmick.
- Reference the specific occasion.
- Emphasize the importance of the topic/subject.

There you have it. Four simple formats you can use to outline any talk, whether it's a two-minute overview or an all-day seminar. Using these tools, you will never be at a loss for words. Never without something to say, and always prepared to say it well.

Grab 'em, Wow 'em

Organizing your presentation is a fairly simple matter, as you can see. What's tough is grabbing them and wowing them.

The opener and closer represent only 25 percent of your presentation, but that 25 percent is critical.

A writer friend tells me about the New York publishing house editor who admonishes her writers that the first chapter sells **this** book to the reader, but the final chapter sells the **next** book. And Jonellen Heckler, novelist and wife of fellow speaking professional Lou Heckler, teaches would-be writers that the first scene of a novel should yank the reader into the story.

Openings and closings are critical for riveting the audience.

For that opening 15 percent, you'll want a real attention getter, a grabber, something that pulls the listener into your

Memorable Closings

We're all in sales, whether we're selling an idea, a product or a service. And the close of our presentation is when we ask for the business, when we make our best case, when we try to close the deal. The close harks back to our purpose, whether it is to inform, inspire, persuade or entertain. Many of the techniques listed in Grabber Openings can be used to create a terrific close.

Remember to close with strength. Get rid of weak words and phrases (think, maybe, apologies). Some appropriate phrases are nevertheless weak: "In closing", "I have one last point to add", even "Thank you". None of these have power.

Another important point: Don't let the audience think about your close until you are ready. Wear your watch with the face on the inside of your wrist, so you can grab a look at the time as you gesture or glance at notes. If you observably look at your watch, you draw attention away from your message.

Great speeches always encapsulate the message in a way people can take with them.

presentation and compels his or her attention.

Humor is good. A story or anecdote is good. Anything that makes the audience sit up and take notice is a good place to begin your talk.

A friend heard a long-time member of Alcoholics Anonymous begin a talk on his years of sobriety with the story of being stopped the night before on suspicion of drunk driving. Turns out his cataracts were the culprit in his erratic driving. So he told the officer who wanted him to take a breath test, "You're about thirty years too late."

A journalist at ESI began one of her presentations with the anecdote of a fresh-faced kid reporter, impatient to write long investigative pieces, who asked what she would have to write about in order to get permission to write longer stories. This editor responded, "Sex. People won't read 60 inches about tax cuts, but they will about sex."

Wouldn't you like to hear the rest of that presentation? I know I would, whether the rest of it is about sex or not.

Then, for that 10 percent at the close of your talk, you want to review your presentation and leave the audience with something memorable, something quotable, something inspiring.

A friend recently eulogized her sister, who died young after ten years in a wheelchair. Our friend closed by saying, "Today, I believe Cindy can walk and I believe she can run. But I don't believe she needs to do either. Because today I believe she can fly."

That's a memorable way to end.

By the way, she started out pretty well, too. Her first words were, "I love happy endings. And what we have tonight is a happy ending."

A writer friend tells me there is no wrong or right way to write anything, that different approaches work for each of us. So you may want to experiment. But here is what works for me. Once I've completed my research and my brainstorming, once I've organized my material around the format I've selected, I always begin by outlining in detail. I never write my speeches, but I begin to rehearse based on the outline I've developed. As I rehearse, I refine, revise, reduce.

Then I take two or three words to characterize my message, my key points, my vignettes. I memorize that outline, using those key words. That way, just in case I need to refer to notes, I can write down those key words and tuck them into a jacket pocket.

Personally, I find it easier to develop the middle, or body of a presentation first. I can zero in on the perfect grabber and isolate a memorable close after I'm clear about the body of my presentation.

Also, although I've said I no longer write out my presentations, I recommend that you do so, especially in the beginning, especially with new material. Although relying on a scripted talk is limiting, most of us need to get the words down on paper.

Feelings vs Facts

You've heard me say more than once that knowing your audience is an important part of your preparation. And here's another instance when understanding who you're speaking to helps you prepare an effective presentation.

No matter who your audience is, know this: *some of the people to whom you are speaking learn and retain based on facts; some hear you best when you address their emotions. Some of us want research, data, numbers. Some of us want a story, an anecdote, a quote.* Even in an audience full of accountants, some will respond best to a story. Even in an audience of novelists, some want to know sales figures.

Your job, as you work on the body of your presentation, is to provide something for both types of listeners. *Support each point you make with both facts and feelings.* We're communicating with each person in the audience, not just those who think the way we think. Give me the sales figures, then tell me the story of the guy who boosted his sales 10 percent by watching the way his daughter ran her lemonade stand. *Facts and figures.*

Head and heart. Humanize, personalize, dramatize. Statistics, study results, information. Draw from both.

Dr. Kay Redfield Jamison, a best-selling author and nationally-recognized expert on mental illness, spoke recently at a local college. The statistics she provided on mental illness, suicide and addiction were compelling. Equally riveting, and probably critical to her success with audience members who yawn over statistics, was the recounting of her personal struggle with bipolar disorder.

Dr. Jamison used that powerful combination of facts and feelings to inform and interest a diverse audience.

Choosing the Right Words

Good communicators can take a complex issue and make it easy to follow. Using discipline, organization and the right words, you can lead an audience to the conclusion you want them to draw.

Cultivate a rich vocabulary. Make it a priority to find the proper word, the perfect word. But never speak over the head of your audience. Don't use $10 words because you won't impress anyone; you'll simply manage to alienate the audience. There is power in simple language, in language that paints a visual picture.

When I tell you there was a fist fight, doesn't that conjure a much more vivid mental picture than telling you there was an altercation? An altercation could mean any number of things, but we all know what a fist fight looks like.

Choose your words, also, for the way they sound when spoken aloud. Some combinations of words flow easily off the tongue, others just manage to trip up your tongue. Other word choices may sound phony for your personality. If a word doesn't come naturally to you, don't use it. Practicing aloud will tell you whether you've made the best choice for a verbal presentation.

Be specific when you choose your words. Don't say we live in a material age, say Americans spend $9 billion on cosmetics every year. Don't talk about a day that history will remember for a long time. Say, as Franklin Roosevelt did on December 7, 1941, "This is a day that will live in infamy."

Check your grammar, your pronunciation. Check word meanings. If you aren't 100 percent confident in these areas, turn to someone who is and ask them to check behind you.

Now Throw Out the Words

You've written it. It's perfect. You know exactly what you want to say and how you want to say it.

You're ready to reduce it all to a few bulleted items on a note card.

You've done all this advance thinking so you won't have to "think on your feet." But you don't want to read a speech, you want to talk to the audience, to converse with them. You want to be polished but natural. So to be the best you can be, you'll want to throw out the written speech, and reduce it to key points on a note card.

I can almost hear you groaning. Write the speech, then throw it out? But how, you might say, can you possibly remember everything you've prepared? The perfect words, the blend of fact and feeling, the grabber opening and memorable close?

The answer is in the next chapter, the final stage in preparing a powerful presentation.

Practice, practice, practice.

Ch. 10 PRACTICE, PRACTICE, PRACTICE

« I don't want to practice
on my audience, I want to
practice in my room. »

This isn't going to take long, because it's the simplest tool for us to use and use well. And we are all equals when it comes to this one; none of us has a leg up here.

Yet no tool is more important—and that's true no matter what your level of talent or expertise.

The next tool in our box is this one: Practice, practice, practice.

Preparation is a habit of excellence. Of course, we'd all like to achieve excellence without the drudgery of practice. We'd like to hit the green every time without spending hours on the driving range. And so would Tiger Woods. We'd like to play the piano well enough to bring the house down at the next holiday party without having to tickle the ivories between performances. Likewise, I'm sure, Billy Joel.

We'd also like to hit a home run from the podium without preparation, without practice.

But without practice, the best we can hope for is a high fly. And we know what happens to the high fly ball. Sometimes it drops into left field for a double, even makes it over the fence in a rare moment of magic. But most of the time it's an easy out.

Think back to high school for a moment. Remember the student body president or the star athlete? The people who, with no effort whatsoever, had the world at their feet. The rest of us, we had to get out there and knock ourselves out just to feel like a member of the club. We had to try harder, do more, just to be in the same room with those folks.

But ten years later, some of those high school stars are still living off their old glory. They haven't changed much. And the old glory has often passed them by, while the rest of us who had to try so hard have plotted a real upward curve on our life graphs.

The point here is that a little bit of skill—in life or in front of an audience—isn't necessarily a blessing. If you can just wing it and be pretty good, you may never be great. Because you've got so little incentive to reach higher, you take it for granted that all the success you want will always be yours. But the truth is, that little bit of success may be the highest curve on your graph, unless you work harder.

So we've got to practice. Practice. Practice.

Getting Organized

It's important to realize that this habit of preparation is a thread that runs through every stage of our presentation. It starts when we first begin to plan our talk, as we organize our thoughts and ideas, as we translate those thoughts into words. To prepare ourselves thoroughly, we plan and organize every part of our presentation—verbal, vocal and visual.

First, the verbal, or the words we choose. As we learned in the previous chapter, we organize our talk. We think about what message we want to convey to the listeners, how we want to launch our talk and how we want to wrap it up. We carefully craft a grabber opener and a power close.

Then we add in how we'll perform those words. Gestures, movements, audio-visual aids, all the small but significant extras that add layers of professionalism to our presentation.

Then we practice. We practice until the words, the gestures, the movements, the inflections are second nature to us. We practice until we don't need notes. We practice until we can maintain eye contact without being distracted, especially during the critical open and close.

Then, when we're feeling sure of ourselves, we can transfer the key points in our presentation to four-by-six note cards.

There's a sticking point for some of us, I know. Some people feel safer in front of an audience if they have their entire speech in front of them. A copy of their speech becomes a safety net, allows them to feel a little more comfortable in an uncomfortable situation.

But I'd like to encourage you to leave that crutch behind. Use the note cards instead, with those key points, or bulleted items, reduced to a few words and reproduced in a large font. Hold those cards in your hand, if you like, although my best recommendation is to leave them on the lectern and refer to them only when necessary. If you have extensive notes or a prepared speech, your eyes will be irresistibly drawn to them. They will diminish your eye contact.

With enough practice, those note cards are the only crutch you need.

I believe that carrying those few reminders instead of your entire speech is a vital step in becoming effective. And here's why: Because *if you carry a scripted copy of your speech, you don't own it. It owns you.*

If that's not reason enough, here's another one. If we carry note cards with key points to the lectern with us, we can then deliver our message, not read a speech. George Plimpton suggests we learn a speech point by point, not word for word. Excellent advice.

Off-the-Cuff Practice

Once we've condensed our message to bullets on note cards, we need to practice some more. Then, when we're comfortable with our ability to deliver our message, we can expand our practice. We can begin to prepare for the more impromptu segments of our presentation.

Many of us must deal with question-and-answer sessions and it may seem that there's no way to prepare for that.

I practice for Q-and-A as thoroughly as I practice the rest of my presentation. I ask friends, family, colleagues to pepper me with questions. If they aren't asking the tough questions, I supply them with a few. I insist that they not let me off the hook. I work until I am well-prepared to think on my feet, to handle the unexpected.

Look at it this way: *I don't want to practice on my audience, I want to practice in my room.*

I always like to know how I will respond to the five toughest questions I can imagine. I like to anticipate worst-case scenarios. And I prepare for them.

Remember David McClelland, who conducts training sessions for schools and colleges? He makes the case for practicing Q-and-A sessions better than I can. One day David arrived to discover that the class didn't want his prepared presentation after all—but a question-and-answer session.

"Thanks to all the practice that I did before the presentation, I felt very comfortable doing an hour-long ad-lib on the specific needs of this group," David says. "As people asked to be shown different capabilities of the software—some of which I had little experience with—I remembered that Ty had told me to restate the question back to the group to gain extra time to think of a proper response. I also remembered to take some small breaks to drink from my water bottle after a difficult question was asked. This also gave me the extra time needed to think of the right answer to the question.

"A little simple planning and practice turned a difficult speaking situation into just another day at the office."

We can all say the same, if we remember to practice.

You'll find the tips David mentioned, and others, in the sidebar on Q-and-A in this chapter.

Remember this: Even if the meeting is informal, prepare for it. Have one great idea in mind. The lead is rarely given, it's taken. And you can take the lead with one great idea. That idea may just surface during your practice.

Any salesperson, manager or leader can measurably improve output (sales closings, productivity, team-building, etc.) if they will simply anticipate their encounters, prepare and practice. That improvement can be dramatic. It can keep the curve on the graph moving up.

Fine-tuning

While the big picture certainly gets better as a result of practice, this is also the time for fine-tuning, for those spit-polish details that take our presentation to the next level. One of those details is timing.

We all need to practice our timing, and to make sure we'll fill—but not run over—the time allotted. Most of us deliver in the range of 110-140 words per minute. But relying on an average doesn't allow for our individual differences. Through practice, you can learn your own pace.

You will also learn that practice makes a difference in the amount of time required to deliver a presentation. At ESI, we find that almost all of our students profit by slowing their delivery. Because for some of us, fear makes us rush. So a nice twenty-minute presentation on paper can turn into a tense ten minutes of rapid-fire delivery.

So practice for the purpose of refining your timing. Figure out if you need to add or delete, expand or condense, slow down or pick up the pace. Look for the right place to do each—times when a quickening of the pace will also quicken the listener's pulse, or when a breather will be appreciated. Remember, anytime any part of our presentation is predictable, we risk boring our listener.

And, yes, you need to practice even if you're preparing for a lengthy presentation, an all-day class for example. There is plenty of time for the unexpected in an all-day session, or even a half day, and practice is the only way you can be sure you have adequate material and the confidence to handle whatever comes up.

Practice is the time, as well, to swing for the fences. To exaggerate our gestures, our voices, our facial expressions. Then, when we're in front of an audience, we'll feel comfortable enough to hit that home run.

Dress Rehearsal

We've talked a lot about how much we can improve our communications skills by using the skills of the actor. An expressive face, vocal variety, purposeful movements, all those tools increase our effectiveness.

Here's another tradition we can borrow from the theater: the dress rehearsal.

You may think this is going to extremes, but try it. It's one of the most effective ways I know to get truly comfortable with your presentation. You've already practiced. You're feeling confident. But this final step will potentially uncover glitches that can knock your legs out from under you on presentation day.

Three or four days before your presentation, put on the clothes you're planning to wear, set up a video camera if you can get your hands on one, and plant yourself in front of a mirror—preferably full-length. Then give it all you've got.

Hit for the fence.

This gives you the opportunity to make adjustments that will increase both your comfort level and your effectiveness. In my years of using this technique, I've discovered that a suit didn't fit as well as I thought, that I was missing a button, even that the right suit was still at the cleaners. I've learned that a different gesture fit more naturally within the context of my presentation than what I'd planned. I've watched the tape and realized that the words I'd chosen came out muddled or awkward.

By engaging in something that makes us all feel a little self-conscious, even a little silly, I have been able to make minor adjustments that created major improvements.

Equally important, this simple little technique enables us, on the day of our presentation, to concentrate on substance instead of style.

Owning the Territory

Now you're comfortable with your message, your words, your gestures, even the clothes and shoes you're going to wear. Sounds like plenty. That ought to be it. Right?

Well, I have one more suggestion for you that makes a profound difference in how smoothly your presentation goes off. I call it owning the territory.

Check out the location ahead of time.

This won't always be feasible, I know. But if you make it a regular part of your routine, it's doable a lot more often than you might realize. Show up the night before, if possible. An hour before, if that's the best you can manage. Get the lay of

the land. Make sure everything is set up as nearly as possible in a way that makes you feel most comfortable and that creates the best arena for successful communication.

Here are some examples of what I mean.

- Is the room set up so that people who come in late or leave early can enter or exit without crossing between you and the audience?

- Is there a lectern, a table, a bank of microphones that become a barrier between you and the audience?

- Is the first row of chairs or tables too close or too far away from you?

- Is everything you need for your audio-visual support there and in working order? Handouts ready? Microphone on?

- Is the room set up awkwardly, perhaps requiring you to turn your back on some members of the audience in order to face others?

- Is the room too dark, too bright? Too cold or too hot?

- Is there a window behind you, offering a distracting view to the audience? Or is the window behind the audience, allowing the sun to blind you? Do blinds or curtains need adjusting?

If you walk into the room where you'll be presenting, imagine yourself making the presentation and look for anything at all that is out of kilter. You'll be surprised how many little things you can find to tweak. Little tweaks that will make a big difference in your ability to connect with your audience.

You may think this sounds a little too nitpicky. Well, remember our friend David McClelland, whose Q-and-A session was saved by a little practice? David has another story, as well.

David had just learned the importance of owning the territory, so he showed up thirty minutes early to get accustomed to the room and to make sure all the electronic equipment was up and running.

"I'm very thankful I learned to arrive early," David says. "As I examined the computer classroom, I discovered that they had not installed my software in this particular room. It would have been very hard to complete the training session without the software on the computers.

"With time to spare, I easily installed the program onto each and every computer."

When you own the territory, you are more comfortable. You are more effective. Your audience is more comfortable. And they are more receptive to your message.

These details should also be addressed, whenever it is possible, with whoever is making arrangements for your

---

Mike on Mics

Speaking into a microphone doesn't simply magnify our voice. Often, it magnifies our fear, as well.

But mics are simply another tool in your toolbox, and one you can put to work for you with a little preparation. Let's talk about the four keys to making a microphone work for you, not against you.

First, preparation. Get to the room early and do the following things. Introduce yourself to the AV people, let them know you realize how important they are to the success of your presentation. Then ask their help. Set the volume levels, adjust the height of the gooseneck on the lectern (between sternum and chin is best). Make sure there's enough mic cable to allow you to make purposeful movements. Ask them to replace the battery in the mic. Don't leave anything to chance.

Second, dress smart. Women must be especially conscious of microphones when they're dressing for a presentation. Jewelry that jingles and clinks can become a real distraction. Strapless or spaghetti strap dresses may be appropriate in certain situations, but they do present a problem with lapel mics. Carry a scarf or shawl or other wrap of some type. Men, be sure to clip your mic very high on your tie or lapel.

Third, pack your own. If you present frequently, consider carrying your own wireless mic for more freedom of movement. They are available for as little as $200 in an electronics store. You can take them anywhere and plug into any PA system. Remember, if you're hiding behind a lectern, you're closing the lid on a big part of your toolbox.

Fourth, always assume the mic is on. That's the worst mistake people make, forgetting that the microphone is on and saying something they didn't want broadcast to the entire room. Remember the George W. Bush faux pas in the 2000 presidential election, when he badmouthed a member of the press?

The microphone is a tool. Make it work for you. Don't let the mic leave you speechless.

— **Mike Furr**
ESI Videographer and faculty member

presentation. Put everything in writing in advance, and ask for confirmation in writing as well. Don't assume anything. Take responsibility yourself for creating a communication-friendly environment.

A key detail to attend to is your introduction. Never assume that the people arranging your presentation have the appropriate material to introduce you. Write your own brief introduction, highlighting the credentials that qualify you to speak on your topic. You'll eliminate mistakes and embarrassment. And although it flies in the face of the modesty some of us have, it is critical for the audience to know that we're someone worth listening to.

One of the checkpoints above mentioned the presence of a lectern or other barrier between you and the audience. I want to pause for a minute and ask you to make note of that point. Some presenters choose to overlook that point, because the idea of presenting without a lectern sounds a little bit threatening to many of us. We can lean on a lectern. We can hang onto it. We can hide our trembling knees behind it. A lectern becomes as much a safety net as that copy of our speech.

Certainly, a lectern is a wonderful thing to speak from, for all those reasons. But chances are the day will come when a lectern will not be available for your presentation. And if you've been using a lectern as a crutch for any of the reasons above, you will suddenly find yourself at a disadvantage. You will suddenly be outside your comfort zone. You'll feel inadequately prepared.

Now, we wouldn't dare teach you to run with a crutch. So I'm going to ask you to break your crutches. From this moment on, come out from behind that lectern. Put your notecards on it, then leave it alone, returning to it only as a touchstone when you want to pause, collect your thoughts, check a fact. Learn to speak without the lectern. It is a barrier between you and the audience, between your presentation skills today and the skills you can have tomorrow, if you are willing.

Remember, as we learned in Chapter Six, your body, your physical presence, is one of the most effective items in your toolbox. Why hide it?

A Level Playing Field

If you practice, you will be ready. You will be effective. You will succeed as a communicator. Practice and preparation are the simple tools we all have available to us, no matter what our skill in other areas. No matter how resonant our voice, no matter how naturally effortless our posture, no matter what kind of smile we have or what kind of eye contact we learn to make—we can all practice, practice, practice.

And if we do pull that one simple tool out of our toolbox, we will have leveled the playing field. Actually, we will be well ahead of 90 percent of our peer group. Because we can all learn, through practice, to make better use of the voice we have, to stand tall, to move effectively, to connect with the audience.

All of our tools become more polished with practice, practice, practice.

Some presenters dread question-and-answer time, but it's actually one of my favorite times in any presentation. I love the interaction with the audience. I love to hear what's on their minds. I especially love it when I get a question I've never heard before.

Of course, the better prepared we are, the better able we are to handle questions. I've already mentioned that I practice Q&A time, asking family and friends to fire questions at me, giving me the opportunity to think on my feet.

A couple of quick thoughts on Q&A sessions:

Don't be afraid to say, "I don't know." Remember our earlier discussion that being vulnerable adds to the effectiveness of our communication? Here's the perfect time to remind the audience that even the most knowledgeable expert doesn't have all the answers and doesn't mind saying so. When I'm faced with this situation, I always promise to find the answer. Then I follow up with a call or note to the questioner, without fail, and without delay.

Another technique that works when you don't have the answer is to ask for input from the audience. This generates tremendous enthusiasm, and often teaches me something that will prove valuable to me, as well.

Answer a broad question with a specific answer and a specific question with a broad answer. Here's an example of what I mean. If someone asks what you believe will happen in the stock market over the next ten years, that's a pretty broad question. Try to zero in on one area, such as tech stocks, or the impact of e-trading. If someone asks how you think the break-up of Microsoft will affect the stock market, pull back and talk in broader terms about how other anti-trust rulings have affected us.

Remember that this is Q&A, not inquisition time. You've agreed to answer questions, not be interrogated. And if you're uncomfortable with what's happening, chances are the audience will be, too. So if I'm getting grilled by someone in the audience, I respond not just to that questioner, but to the entire audience. I also try to keep in mind that there is a difference between a tough question and a hostile question. If I think of a question as hostile, I may respond with hostility. So I maintain as pleasant a demeanor as possible in responding to unpleasant questions. I often say, "I'm glad you asked that." For more on tough questions, you'll find everything you need in Chapter Eleven.

Don't be distracted by inappropriate questions. An example. Alice May, a friend who has written a book on marital problems, was recently asked in a forum if she was a Christian. Now, this was not a religious presentation, but some of her responses to other questions had revealed a reliance on spiritual solutions in healing troubled relationships. Of course, answering the question with either a yes or a no was bound to put off someone in the audience, and thus detract from her ability to provide helpful guidance to everyone there. One alternative would have been to suggest that she and the questioner discuss that matter later, in private. Another, and the response Alice chose, was to explain that she found it to be most helpful if she didn't discuss her specific religious beliefs, so that all listeners were free to identify how her suggested solutions worked within the framework of their own personal beliefs. Her response was well-received and she moved on quickly to the next question. Don't allow yourself to be pulled off track by questions that don't fit your message.

Always repeat the question. And it's a good idea to paraphrase it as you do so. This clarifies the question for both you and the other members of the audience, making sure everyone is on the same page. It also gives you the chance to think about your answer. Another way to pause and consider is to take a drink from your water bottle.

If the question is important, there's nothing wrong with planting it. Ask someone ahead of time to bring up a certain point if you want to make sure the question gets asked.

Keep the energy level high. If questions aren't coming quickly, wrap it up. Don't linger, trying to drag out the last question on someone's mind. Instead, draw things to a close while the questions are still coming in strong. Comment that there is time for one more question, but that you'll be available after the session for further discussion.

Prepare a second close. Craft another powerful closing comment or two to follow a question-and-answer session. This brings the energy level of the meeting back up, leaving the audience feeling enthusiastic, charged up.

Ch. 11 — THE HOSTILE AUDIENCE

« When we demonstrate our respect for the audience and their beliefs or feelings, we are neutralizing the hostility. »

Let's get honest. Not all audiences are friendly.

Most are. But we all have those rare occasions when we must communicate with a group or individual who won't be receptive to our message—in politics, employee-management relations, community decision-making, certainly when it comes to family issues.

And any audience we address, even the friendliest, potentially has the guy who doesn't want to be there; who doesn't believe in what we're saying; who tumbled out of the wrong side of the bed that morning and is still ticked off at the world.

In the overwhelming number of cases, the audience is on our side. Everyone out there wants us to succeed. But eventually most of us will be asked to make a presentation that isn't going to be popular with some or even most members of the audience. Or we'll look out and see that one disgruntled face.

So what do we do when somebody—or a lot of somebodies—in the audience is clearly not rooting for us?

Yes, the hostile audience and the unpleasant audience member are out there. But with a little preparation, and a few adjustments in our own thinking, we can be prepared for the unfriendly audience.

The Black Hole of Negativity

First, let's talk about the isolated case, that person in the audience who isn't smiling back when you make eye contact with him or her.

Do not allow that person to become the focus of your attention.

It's that simple—and awfully tough.

I know the urge to win him or her over. To send all your charm, your best smile, your most intense eye contact in that direction. To talk directly to that person. We've all given in to that urge from time to time.

And the result is deadly.

When we direct our focus onto the negative person in the audience, our energy level shifts. All our energy is funneled into the black hole of one person's negativity. Ultimately, *we're no longer presenting out of enthusiasm and passion, but out of fear and negativity.*

Focus on your entire audience, especially those whose enthusiasm feeds your own. As a friend says, "Feed the dog you want to win."

Next, recognize that there's a 99 percent certainty this person's hostility has nothing to do with you. You may be the focus of his or her animosity, but the underlying reason is almost always something else. The boss. The spouse. The promotion that went to somebody else.

So don't take it on. Don't shoulder this guy's problems and make them yours. Imagine a neon sign on his forehead, flashing on and off: Unhappy person. Unhappy person. Unhappy person. Not: Hates me. Hates me. Hates me.

When you can picture that neon sign, it should create a little compassion in you. And where there's compassion, it's hard to carry fear or lack of confidence. Where there's compassion, you can smile and move on. Smile and move on to the other members of the audience who are receptive to your message. The people you **can** reach today.

Another type of apparent hostility to be aware of—and to be careful not to react to—is the question that appears hostile. We addressed that in the previous chapter when we discussed preparing for question-and-answer sessions. But here's another helpful awareness: often participants with a question that comes across as hostile are simply trying to show command of the subject, to demonstrate their knowledge. They want attention, and one easy way to get it is to rattle or disagree with or one-up the speaker. Handled well, such a circumstance can fill their need without sidetracking the discussion.

For example, a response such as, "That's a great question. Here's one way of looking at that..."

You haven't discounted the question or comment, but you also haven't placed the power or the direction of the program in the hands of a difficult person.

Remember, if you play to the hostile audience member, you're losing your focus. Your focus becomes your attempt to make that person happy. And it should be delivering your message to the people who want what you have to offer. If you keep that focus, you may even find that you can turn around the one unhappy soul in the audience.

Re-establishing the Connection

Again, let me make the point that the truly hostile audience is rare. But it does happen and it's important to be mentally prepared for it.

The good thing about presenting to a hostile audience is that we're usually aware going in that we'll be dealing with a tough crowd. If it's political, if it's an inflammatory issue, we know up front what to expect. In those circumstances, sometimes the best we can ask of them is to give us the opportunity to explain our views.

And we begin by giving respect to their views.

When we demonstrate our respect for the audience members and their beliefs or feelings, we are neutralizing the hostility as much as possible. And we're opening the door to a sense of fair play by being fair ourselves.

I try to think of the hostile audience in this way. When hostility is present, emotions are involved. And as a presenter, my responsibility is to understand and respect those emotions. I don't have to agree with them, but I need to try to put myself in their shoes and have some empathy for their circumstances. I owe it to them and to myself to anticipate their emotional responses and find ways to address their worries and concerns.

I also owe them honesty. In a difficult circumstance, that is sometimes the only thing I can offer that demonstrates my respect for them even if we view things differently.

Let's look at how Joan Zimmerman, CEO of Southern Shows, Inc., handled a tough political audience a few years ago. She had been asked to speak to the North Carolina House of Representatives against a bill that would have assigned pay scale equivalencies. Now, many women were in favor of the bill and the audience was packed with those women. They were quite vocal in their criticism of the people speaking against the bill.

"I was not relishing my turn on the hot spot," Joan recalls. "I knew I needed to establish credibility—this was an intelligent group of women—and the fact that I did understand their position.

"But I also needed them to understand why I was opposed to this bill."

So Joan, in the interest of connecting with her audience and acknowledging respect for their views, abandoned her technical speech. Instead, she began by outlining her own record of support for women's issues.

Then and only then did she have the credibility to explain why she did not support this particular bill.

The results were spectacular.

"Not a boo. Not a hiss. Not a heckle," Joan recalls. "One woman stood and said, 'Thank you for all you've done.'"

Quite a turnaround, wouldn't you say?

And essentially, all Joan did was use honesty, respect for the other side's opinions, and modify her original plan in anticipation of her audience's viewpoint. Instead of making that audience her enemy, she first focused on their common ground. And that made them receptive to her opposing opinion in a way that treating them as adversaries would never have accomplished.

Regardless of the severity of the question or reaction from the audience, I always coach people to treat the question as merely tough, but not adversarial. Because viewing it as adversarial encourages you to go on the attack as well. And *once you go on the attack, you are encouraging the audience to choose sides. They won't always choose your side.* You've raised a high barrier between you and the audience.

So always, at all costs, avoid becoming a part of a confrontation. You will never win when you become a hostile player in a confrontation with someone in your audience.

When it comes to handling the irate confrontation, however, the most important step I can take is to lower the level of emotionalism. No one can listen to different ideas when emotions are raging. Here are some thoughts about bringing emotions below the boiling point.

Ask this question of the challenging individual: Has my company or my cause done something to upset you? If so, please tell me about it. Then allow them to vent.

Ask if there is something you personally have done. This helps the person identify where the anger is coming from.

And in both cases, listen to what's being said. Really listen. Use the active listening techniques described in Chapter Five. And when the individual is finished, say, "I don't blame you for feeling that way."

Can you see how this will help you connect even with the hostile audience member, and perhaps the hostile audience as a whole?

What this comment does is bring you back to the same side. You will have provided a safety valve for the emotion building up in an individual or an audience. Then you can re-introduce logic.

Don't Believe the Hostility

Ultimately, as my mentor Bill Gove says, "We must be responsible for our own behavior, but we cannot be responsible for the actions of an individual, or the crowd."

If you've prepared well for your presentation, as we suggest in Chapter Ten, you're well-equipped to handle objections, hostility, those who won't agree with you. You've got no reason to run from that hostility. Open the door for objections. Invite their skepticism. And deal with it straightfor-wardly. You're prepared, remember? You've rehearsed respons-es to all the tough questions. You're on solid ground. Don't be afraid to step out there.

Don't believe in the one hostile face in the crowd. Believe in the members of the audience who are signaling their receptiveness. Don't even believe in an entire roomful of glaring faces. Believe in your message.

Believe in yourself.

NEVER AGAIN BE CONTROLLED BY FEAR

« You can get rid of the voice in your head that says you can't do it. »

If you're reading this book to get rid of your fear of speaking in front of others, you're in the wrong place.

In my experience, that isn't possible. And it isn't even desirable, for reasons I'll get into later.

What you can do is *change the way you think about fear.*

I'm not going to give you a quick fix for your fear. The instant prescription that will eliminate your fear forever. What I am going to give you is, I believe, much more valuable than that. What I am going to give you is a way to change the way you think about—and therefore the way you react to—fear.

I've seen this process transform people, their lives and their careers and their sense of self. And you can do what they do: You can get rid of the voice in your head that says you can't do it.

Sure you can. You've got the tools. And one of them, believe it or not, is the very fear you're allowing to hold you back.

Well, never again. In this chapter, we're going to shine a light on your fear. A light so bright fear need never have power over you again. Fear won't control you; you'll control it.

All God's Children Got Fear

Yep, every one of us.

Don't believe it? Let's talk about President John Kennedy, for starters.

Most of us have heard about the day he urged us, "Ask not what your country can do for you; ask what you can do for your country."

I remember it. His voice rang with authority. He connected with his audience, the American people, so powerfully that he is still quoted, decades later.

And behind the lectern, his knees were shaking.

JFK's knees were shaking.

A friend of mine in Charlotte was a Secret Service agent during the Kennedy presidency. Every time JFK got behind the lectern, my friend Andy was standing right behind him. And as the young president juggled tough questions with ease and won us over with his confident smile and the assurance behind his words, his knees were shaking. Every time.

Did his fear make him less effective in communicating with us? History has already judged that one for us, wouldn't you say?

We all have adrenaline. Kennedy and Oprah and Brokaw. Even Old Big Deal, and I've been presenting to one group or another virtually every day for, well, more than a few years.

For the past twenty years, as Pat and I have coached those who want to become master communicators, we find that every single person experiences some kind of fear, ranging from mild discomfort to sheer panic.

In fact, experience has taught us that those who don't raise their hand when we ask who has fear are either afflicted with an excess of bravado or they're just plain...well, I hesitate to call anybody a liar. But some of us have a more intimate relationship with the truth than others.

Let me say this again: Everybody—not just you, everybody—feels fear, unless they're neurotic, in denial or just plain crazy. This I know: under the right circumstances all of us will feel fear when speaking.

And that fear holds us back. Keeps us from achieving all that we could. Inhibits relationships. Controls our lives. Yes, fear controls our lives. We've all read the survey results: fear of speaking in public is at the top of the list. We're more afraid of speaking in public than we are of dying.

Every time we coach, we see people who have stopped their careers cold rather than stand before others and present their ideas. We see people who don't take leadership roles in their areas of passion; who can't share their talents with others;

who can't confront the difficulties of everyday relationships. All because of fear.

Fear. We've all got it.

It's a natural response.

Don't we all jump when we hear an unexpected loud noise? Standing to present is the same kind of thing. It gives us a rush of adrenaline. And that makes us uncomfortable, gives us a feeling of dis-ease. For some folks, that natural response is even more intense—they'll have full-blown panic attacks, where they can't breathe, their hearts race or they feel chest pains. Their fear is enormous, the consequences real.

Let me tell you something. After learning to change the way they think about fear, in the same ways we'll discuss in this book, those folks find their fear no longer controls them. Some even walk away and never have another panic attack. Now, the psychologists will tell you that's not possible, that it takes years of intensive therapy to rid yourself of a panic attack.

But that's not our experience.

In our experience, all it takes to change our reactions to fear is a willingness to change the way we think and walk through that fear.

Those 'AHA!' Moments

One of the great **Aha!** moments for ESI attendees comes in the first hour. Everyone introduces themselves, doing a 2-minute impromptu presentation on who they are and why they're there. When it's over, they all heave a great sigh of relief and almost always admit to being terribly nervous. All of them.

From that, people realize two things.

First, they see they have not been singled out by God to suffer this horrible fear. Until then, most of them think they're the only ones. Suddenly they realize everyone has it, to one degree or another. *They are not alone.*

Next, they realize that they couldn't see fear in the others. And others didn't see the fear in them.

Aha! We can feel the fear without being shut down by it. *Our fear doesn't necessarily show.*

For most folks, that's a profound realization.

One of our graduates was a research chemist from Nigeria, whose fear of speaking grew worse after coming to the U.S. because he realized his accent made it difficult for others to understand him. He took speech therapy to improve his enunciation and soften his accent, but it did nothing to lessen his fear.

Then he came to me, and not exactly enthusiastically. In fact, I think "reluctantly" is the word he used.

"Little did I know that this was going to bring a great change to my life," he said. "For once, I realized that fear is a peculiar experience shared by even the most sought-after speakers. Most surprising was hearing fellow associates whom I thought had no fear of public speaking get up and say that they were there in training to lose fear of public speaking."

This research chemist and others in our classes are beginning to understand that fear is normal. And whatever your degree of fear, you can reduce it to a manageable size.

One of our toughest cases was a young female executive for a large company, a talented and promising woman who was fast-tracking her way to the top—except for one small drawback. She couldn't present. Couldn't express herself in a board meeting or a staff training session or a sales presentation. So her boss asked her to attend ESI.

The woman signed up. Then cancelled. Once, twice, three times.

The only reason she didn't cancel a fourth time was her boss's ultimatum: complete the course or else.

She was deathly ill on day one.

And on the third day, she tells us, she felt as if she'd set down a heavy burden she'd been carrying most of her life. Because Linda had to get up and speak, introduce, present, she was forced to confront her worst fear—that she would humiliate herself as she had done once before.

You see, at the age of thirteen, Linda had a piano recital.

When she reached the stage and sat at the piano, fear gripped her and she forgot every note she had been practicing for months. She experienced that worst-case-scenario all performers and presenters dread. She went completely blank and could not proceed. She told herself if she got off that stage alive, she'd never put herself in that position again.

Her fear had been so strong it even blocked the information that could have salvaged her recital: the sheet music was stored in the piano bench.

The event that triggered Linda's fear had happened twenty-five years earlier, but it was as fresh in her mind as if it had happened yesterday. And it continued to control her life.

Until she accepted our challenge to look her fear squarely in the eye. We shone a light on it, and gave her the opportunity to walk through her fear, little by little, step by step. And on the third day of coaching she stood up and performed as if she had done it all her life.

She was calm. She was effective. She was free from her fear.

Not because she no longer had the fear. But because she had learned to manage it, instead of allowing it to manage her.

You can do the same thing. You can learn to manage your fear, rather than continuing to let it manage you.

You can stop viewing your fear as a hurdle and begin to see it, instead, as a launching pad.

Reasons for Fear

Our ESI alum who lived for twenty-five years off an old fear isn't alone. Memories of failure haunt huge numbers of people who feel they can't present successfully.

Falling on our faces once can put the fear in us for eternity.

I remember years ago seeing an interview with actors Gregory Peck and Charlton Heston, certainly two of the most respected leading men in the history of cinema. The interviewer asked a question—a single question—about their most humiliating experience as a performer. Both these accomplished and, to all appearances, enormously confident performers spent the next hour recounting all their professional failures and embarrassments. All their failures, but not a single success.

So past failures get their teeth into us. They become a major contributor to fear.

Let's look at the other reasons we are fearful. Try to identify which ones apply to you.

We Entertain Ourselves with What Ifs: You know what I mean. We write the worst scripts imaginable, horror stories of communications failures worse than anything even Stephen King could imagine. What if we fall going up the steps? What if we faint? What if they laugh at us? What if they see us for what we really are?

Guess what? If you stand up in front of groups often enough, sooner or later you're going to find yourself facing some kind of disaster or another.

One of our ESI alums, Peg, was called in at the last minute to conduct a business writing seminar for the American Institute of Banking. All the classroom materials were provided, she had everything she needed except adequate time to prepare. So Peg was nervous. Very nervous. She had two hours to fill that first night and ample material to work with.

Changing Your Beliefs about Fear

Here is the truth about fear:

- Fear only controls us when we give in to it.
- The simple task of walking through our fear—doing what we fear, then doing it again—transforms our fear into courage.
- We change our negative, limiting thoughts by behaving in a manner contrary to those thoughts. When we act as if we have courage often enough, we wake up one morning and discover that we do have courage.
- Fear is a habit. We establish a new habit by faking it 'til we make it.
- Our fear rarely shows. And when it does show, it shows less than we think.
- Fear is rooted in perfectionism. Accept your humanness and remember that vulnerability is an asset in effective communication.
- You will survive even your worst-case-scenario. Preparation and practice will see us through anything.
- Fear is normal.
- Fear can be transformed into one of our greatest tools: Energy. More on that in Chapter Fourteen.

"But I realized twenty minutes into the class that I'd already used up three-fourths of the material designated for that night," Peg said. "I could see ninety minutes stretching out in front of me with nothing to say to this room full of bankers. I felt the panic rising in me. And I could tell that any minute this panic was going to start to show. I was going to look like a fool and that, for me, was my worst case scenario."

As soon as she realized she was in danger of truly panicking, Peg knew she needed time. Time to regroup. Time to calm down. She assigned a writing exercise. Gave the bankers fifteen minutes to complete it. And while they worked, she first took a few minutes to calm herself. Then she was able to plan the rest of that first night's class.

"When those fifteen minutes were up, I was okay again. I had regained control of myself. And nobody in the room had an inkling that I'd been so close to losing it."

One of my most memorable experiences also started out as a disaster.

I was speaking at a Chamber of Commerce awards dinner in a hotel ballroom so crowded the fire marshal would've shut us down if he'd happened upon us. The tables were crowded

---

Some Thoughts About Diminishing Fear

- Develop a personal mantra or affirmation that cuts the power of your fear. Phrase it in present tense, as if it were already true. Repeat it daily. Look yourself in the mirror and say the words. "What I feel is normal and has no power over me. It does not hold me back or limit me in any way." Or, "Fear is an old habit. My new habit is confidence."
- Practice relaxation techniques regularly, not just before big presentations.
- Talk about your fear to people you can trust.
- Slow down. If your heart is racing, slow down all the physical responses you can — voice, movements. Take the time to make eye contact.
- Stand tall and breathe correctly (Chapter Eight), which will strengthen your voice and eliminate the quivers.
- Smile.
- Practice, practice, practice.
- Turn your fear into energy (Chapter Fourteen).

together and the waiters were doing an admirable job squeezing between us to clear the tables. As I was introduced, I sprang up from my chair…just as a waiter came by with a tray of half-finished spinach salads, soup bowls and strawberry shortcake remains.

The tray caught me just over the left eye. I landed flat on my back, as did the tray and the waiter.

I was momentarily dazed, had food all over my blue suit and thought, This is not going to be one of my great days.

But when I stood in front of the audience a few moments later, I was greeted with a standing ovation before I even opened my mouth. Bottom line, the audience and I made a powerful connection because of, not in spite of, the incident. Remember the mention of vulnerability in Chapter Three. Boy, did it work for me here. As a matter of fact, the presentation was so successful I tracked the waiter down afterward and jokingly asked if he wanted to go on the road with me.

He said he'd have to decline, that he wasn't sure he could stand the pressure of show biz.

The lesson in both my story and Peg's is that, even if the worst thing you can imagine happens, you can survive it.

Believe me, you can survive it.

We Have Less Power: Let's say you're presenting to a roomful of people who know more about the subject of your presentation than you do. Or let's say you're presenting to a group of people who have more authority or power than you have—company executives, for example, or prospective buyers. Is there a level of intimidation or insecurity? Of course there is.

If, however, you are the one with power, your fear automatically goes down.

We call this position power—your perception that you have less power for some reason—and knowing what you're dealing with can dissipate your fear. Once you name the fear, it's suddenly less formidable.

This is one example of what we call situational fear. Another one is:

New Circumstances: During my years in broadcasting, anytime I went to a new market I became fearful again. But after I'd been on the air for a while and created a relationship with the audience, the fear went away.

The first time I spoke professionally outside my usual broadcast coverage area was in the mid-60s, for the Alabama League of Municipalities, in Montgomery, Alabama. Lurleen Wallace was governor and hers was a name that had garnered much national attention. But this cool kid from North Carolina was no stranger to celebrities and I went into the situation with so much confidence some might have called me cocky.

When I actually arrived in this strange location, surrounded by people who didn't know me from my local TV exposure, this cool cat turned into a nearly panic-stricken kitten. Not because my skills were different, but because my circumstances were different and that made what was going on in my head different.

That anxiety over new circumstances will almost always crop up, no matter how long we've been at this or how long our resume of presentations.

For example, I remember the first time I charged $1000 to speak. I was scared, well, spitless. A major corporation in Harrisburg, PA, had sent a private jet to pick me up. I was to speak to the chairman and senior officials of one of the world's most successful financial holding companies.

The closer I got to presentation time, the more I was filled with doubt. What in the world could I say that was worth a thousand dollars? On that particular night, I allowed fear to manage me instead of me managing the fear. My humor went away. My timing, my smile, my ability to connect with the audience. My toolbox snapped shut. The applause that night was polite at best. Done in by new circumstances, and the fear that created.

Lack of Preparation: One of the most common—and most easily controlled—reasons for nervousness is that we haven't rehearsed. We know we're ill-prepared, we know we don't know as much as we could/should, we know a million things could go wrong and we haven't got a game plan for any of them.

Remember my Alabama League of Municipalities experience, when a new set of circumstances and people had my fear roaring to life? Guess what happened that day? I was great. All my tools appeared to have abandoned me, but I got through it and nobody knew I had a dry mouth and sweaty palms and Jell-O for knees.

Why? Because I had practiced and practiced and everything I needed came to me because it was second nature to me by then. My practice carried me through.

And lack of practice will leave you flapping in the breeze. Maybe not everytime. But often enough that you'll always have that nagging...fear.

Overreacting to Normal Physical Responses: Cam Marston, one of our ESI faculty, reminds our attendees that the physical responses our bodies experience when we stand to speak are a natural reaction to what we perceive to be a threatening situation.

"It all dates back to the days when we lived in caves," Cam says. "In any threatening encounter, one of us wasn't going to live. And nature gave us some specific tools to deal with those circumstances. Blood rushes to our muscles, to prepare us either to fight or flee.

"When we stand up to speak, the same thing happens. We feel threatened. Blood rushes to our muscles, in the way nature intended. But we feel that natural response and become even more fearful. We begin to shake because our muscles are pumped with blood and we start to wonder if we're going to keel over and suddenly we're really reacting.

"And all those physical reactions mean is that we're ready. Ready for a challenge."

There's one more major contributor to our fear. It's probably my biggest personal obstacle. So big, I'm going to give it a chapter all its own.

I think of it as the voice of Be Perfect in my head. More realistically, I ought to call it Perfect Nonsense.

Relaxation Techniques

Paying attention to the physical aspects of our nervousness pays off in a big way. By borrowing tools from yoga,
from biofeedback, from meditation, we can calm our
bodies and our minds.

Begin by tensing all your muscles, one by one, then loosening them.

Begin with your toes. Curl them tightly. Hold that for a count of five. Then
relax them. Feel and appreciate the difference.

Then move up to your calves, your thighs, your stomach muscles. Clench
your fists, then let them relax. In privacy, before you enter the room,
tighten every muscle in your face. Make the worst frown you can
imagine, purse your lips as tightly as you can. Lilias Folan, a yoga instructor for public TV and a top-notch communicator herself, calls it making a
prune face. Hold that prune face, then let it go. Allow the tension to drain
out of you as you release each tensed muscle.

You can also watch your breathing, and use it to generate calm
assurance. Breathe deeply, into the diaphragm, not just into the chest. Fill
your tummy with breath, then empty it slowly. Do it three times. In
through the nose, out through the mouth. Make an audible, sighing
sound as you release the breath.

And imagine, as you do, that you're gently blowing out your tension,
your nervousness, your fears. Then breathe in calm, confidence, positive
energy. Fill yourself with it, then release your breath again, and with it,
all the fear and tension.

Ch.
13

PERFECT NONSENSE

« Doing our best is an attainable goal; being perfect isn't. »

I am filled with Be Perfect. Never mind that I know better; a part of me that can't be satisfied wants to be perfect every time.

How many of you listen to these voices in your head:

They're not going to like the way I look.

They're not going to like what I say.

I'm not as clever as the last person.

I'm the oldest (or the youngest) person in the room. Or the only woman or minority or Southerner.

When I'm listening to those voices, where is my focus? It's on **me**. Not on the people around me, the people who have come to hear my message, the people who are writing my paycheck that day. On me. And if I could focus all that attention and energy on my audience, guess what would happen?

My fear would diminish.

Because I would no longer be consumed by Be Perfect.

The fact is, I've never been perfect. I'll never be perfect. *So if my benchmark is to be perfect, I'll fail every time.* But what if my benchmark, instead, is to be the best I can be at this moment?

For everyone we coach, we try to extinguish that Be Perfect nonsense. Be Perfect is an impossible taskmaster. It's not that we try to excuse less than your best, it's that we do not demand perfection in what we do. Doing our best is an attainable goal; being perfect isn't. One assures failure. The other, with lots of work behind it, creates success.

Being the Best We Can

Unlearning the belief that perfectionism is a reasonable standard isn't easy. Especially for women, Pat reminds me, for whom physical perfection is sometimes seen as a requirement for those in the limelight.

"We have to keep reminding ourselves that we don't have to be perfect," Pat says. "But there are so many things that can go wrong for a woman. Lipstick on our teeth, a broken heel, a run in our stocking, obvious things."

Now, sometimes people come to us for coaching and hear us saying they need to give up the drive to be perfect and assume we're suggesting they settle for sub-standard performance. Far from it.

Don't confuse excellence with perfection!

We always encourage excellence, and do everything we can to coach our students in the skills that will help them attain personal excellence. But the drive for perfection is a barrier to excellence.

If everything has to be perfect, more often than not we will be disappointed with even the highest performance. But if we hold as our standard being the very best, we still have high expectations of ourselves. We have an accomplishable goal.

Sports gives us some good examples of what I'm talking about. Is Tiger Woods excellent? You bet! Is he perfect? Far from it! Sometimes he's below par on a given hole, sometimes he's even over par. But he doesn't make a hole in one his goal every time he tees off. If that's what he aimed for, he wouldn't be marching toward the history books in the world of professional golf. He'd be a frustrated hacker.

Mark McGwire gave up perfection, which in baseball would be a base hit each time at bat. Instead, he became a record-setting home run hitter. But he also has a high number of strike-outs. Because he's willing to give up striving for impossible perfection, he can seek to do his very best.

As long as we hold up perfection as our aim, we will play not to lose rather than playing to win.

Have you done that? Played is safe to avoid making a mistake, to avoid looking foolish? And in doing so, turned your back on exciting opportunities, challenges that could have taken you to the heights? Have you been so braced against failure that you failed to reach for success?

All in the name of Be Perfect.

All in the name of the impossible goal of perfectionism.

I'd like to suggest a different goal. Not perfection. And not playing it safe.

How about working, instead, toward becoming the best you can be, even if you take a tumble along the way?

Here's the way I look at it. I'm not going to learn to swim by waiting around the edge of the pool for the moment when I'll get it perfect. I have to jump in, splash around, swallow a few gulps of water, attempt a weak dog-paddle. I have to be willing to risk sinking halfway across the pool or I'll never work up the stamina or technique to make it the length of the pool. If I'm going to learn to swim, I must accept that I won't get it perfect the first time.

I must learn to be satisfied with making mistakes and building on those mistakes and calling it progress.

Progress, not perfection, that's what we encourage in the people we coach. Can you do better today than you did the day before? Can you set a goal that is reasonable and congratulate yourself for making progress toward that goal? Can you feel good about your accomplishments? About success in increments?

If not, you're too wrapped up in Be Perfect.

And it will work against you. Be Perfect creates rigidity, paralysis, lack of passion. All the things that can wreck our ability to connect with an audience.

Be Perfect is the number one contributor to emotionally crippling fear.

Managing Fear

So, having unmasked the demon of Be Perfect, let's look once again at our fear. Let's recognize that all the reasons we experience fear are ours to control. All of them are manageable, now that we've looked them in the eye.

If we're all fearful and fear is natural and we don't have to be perfect in order to be effective, what do we do about our fear?

We've already done the most important, the most effective thing we can do to rob fear of its power. We've shone a light on it. We've come to understand it. We've unmasked it as one of those classroom bullies who only has power over us if we permit it.

In the last chapter, we suggested *walking through our fear as a powerful tool in disarming that fear.* We also said a key to controlling fear instead of allowing it to control us is to *change our beliefs about fear.* We outlined a few truths about fear. Let's look at a few more. Then let's pack those truths, those new beliefs, into our toolbox, turn them into concrete tools we can use in keeping fear whittled down to a manageable size.

What are the truths about fear?

We need not fear imperfection. We can be powerful though imperfect. We can be our best but we don't have to be perfect in order to be an effective communicator.

We will experience some level of discomfort when making a presentation. It's okay and it's normal.

A few simple techniques help us get through those physical reactions. The Coach Speaks in this chapter and the last offer some effective techniques for managing our fear and our physical reactions.

But first and foremost, accept that your nervousness is normal. Besides...

We look more comfortable than we feel. Our perceptions about ourselves aren't always accurate. We feel nervous so we think we look it, but the truth is most of us don't show our nerves.

Confidence and nervousness aren't mutually exclusive; you can feel nervous on the inside but still have confidence.

This brings up an important bit of advice: Don't shoot yourself in the foot by acknowledging your fear to your audience and chances are they'll never know. *Never tell the audience you're nervous.* Never tell them you haven't had time to think about what you're planning to say. When you do that, you create fear in them, fear that you'll fail, fear that they'll have to witness your failure. Don't create that reality for them. Because we look in charge. And that makes us far more effective and powerful than we give ourselves credit for.

We can compensate for our fear by coming prepared. We can practice, practice, practice. And even in our worst nightmares, that preparation will kick in and save us from a poor performance.

Don't believe it?

Let me tell you about the time I almost walked off the stage at Radio City Music Hall.

In 1984, I was the Thursday morning kick-off speaker for the annual Million-Dollar Roundtable meeting held for the top three percent in the insurance industry. The expectations for each speaker were huge. I'd been told I had thirty-five minutes. Thirty-eight and I got the hook.

In my practice the night before, I realized what I planned to say was fifty-three minutes long. This created some urgency to do major editing. I worked well into the night, editing and practicing the new message. I practiced so long and hard, I showed up at Radio City Music Hall on two hours sleep.

Now, the stage hands told me three times—three times, mind you—that they had dropped the orchestra pit to clean it following a performance by the orchestra which had opened the day's session. They told me precisely how far I could walk without walking right off the stage.

Well, I delivered my opening lines, the audience was incredibly responsive and I was fired up. In an attempt to create greater intimacy with this huge audience, I began to inch forward on the stage. The next thing I knew, I looked down to see that my toes were literally hanging over the edge of the stage. I was looking down three stories to where the rest of the stage was being cleaned.

Somehow, my practice had been so thorough that I continued to deliver my message. But my body froze. I couldn't move a muscle to back myself up to a safer spot. All I could do was stand stark still until someone realized what had happened and raised the stage.

But my practice enabled me to keep delivering my message. What could have been a calamity wasn't—and my practice kicked in to save the presentation.

Bobby Knight, the volatile former basketball coach from Indiana, told his teams, "In practice I want you to think; in performance I want you to play from instinct."

And you will, if you practice. Practice. Practice.

We can put the focus on the audience rather than on ourselves. When the focus is on self, communications can and usually do fail; when the focus is on others, enormous opportunities open up.

The question to ask yourself before you get up to speak is not, "Will they like me?" or "Will they think I know what I'm talking about?" Instead, try this little bit of self-talk. "What I have to say is valuable. I want to share it with others. How can I do that most effectively? How can I be sure they learn this important topic or enjoy these funny stories?"

Then we can reinforce that connection by seeking a positive response from the audience as quickly as possible.

Progress, Not Perfection

Always think in terms of making progress, not seeking perfection. Aim for excellence, which comes over time, not overnight.

- Can you do better today than you did the day before?
- Can you set a goal that is reasonable and congratulate yourself for making progress toward that goal?
- Can you feel good about your accomplishments?
- Can you learn from mistakes rather than beating yourself over the head with them?
- Can you inventory your accomplishments, assessing both the shining moments and the areas that need improvement?

We can ask for audience feedback, for raised hands, for a verbal response, for a group activity. The sooner we can get a positive response from the audience, the quicker our anxiety level drops tremendously.

And getting positive feedback from our audience is pretty simple, because of this basic truth:

The audience is on our side. The audience rarely wants nor needs all the power we give them. Sometimes we're in an adversarial relationship with our audience, but not often. Most of the time, they want to like us. They want to think we're smart. They want us to be in control. They want us to be entertaining and exciting. They will meet us more than halfway, most of the time.

So What?

Now, none of this is a guarantee that you'll never fail again. You probably will. We all do. And that brings me to a little something I use whenever I'm especially consumed with fear, with Be Perfect.

I listen to my introduction, take in the applause and say to myself, "So what?"

So what? So what if they don't like me? So what if this isn't a life-changing event for them? So what if I don't provide all the information they expected? So what if they aren't entertained or enlightened? So what if they yawn? So what if they discover I'm just human? So what if I lose my voice and have to take a break?

So what?

I don't give the members of my audience or the board or the conference room or the family around the dining room table a power they don't want to use. The power to judge me or belittle me or destroy me.

One of my most respected colleagues in the business of speaking has given me a new way to think of my fear, one that I pass along to everyone I coach. And I hear from them that it changes their entire perspective on fear.

Imagine yourself stepping up to the lectern to deliver a message. What are you feeling? Rapid heartbeat, sweaty palms, rubber knees, tornado tummy.

Now what are you going to call that? Are you going to feed negativity into that situation and call those reactions fear?

What if you had another way to look at those feelings?

Imagine, instead, that you're like a great stallion. Champing at the bit. Ready to leap out of the gate. Your heart is pounding, too. Your knees are quivering with anticipation. Maybe your stomach is in knots.

Are you afraid?

Or do you have racehorse nerves?

Broadway star and communication coach Dorothy Sarnoff calls those physical reactions racehorse nerves. Natural. Inevitable. And guess what else?

Necessary to deliver the best performance you are capable of.

Do you think that horse is going to win if he's apathetic? Laid back? Complacent? Not on a bet.

And neither are you.

If you want to be a winner, the most effective communicator you are capable of being, you're going to need to put your racehorse nerves to work for you. And you can generate those racehorse nerves (which I also like to call energy) through your fear.

Remember my Alabama League of Municipalities presentation? New audience, new location. Those folks didn't know Ty

More Truths About Fear

- If perfection is our benchmark, we will fail every time. Aim instead for progress.
- We can be powerful though imperfect; therefore we need not fear imperfection.
- We can feel nervous on the inside but still have confidence.
- We can compensate for fear with thorough preparation.
- We can focus on the audience rather than our own ego.
- The audience is on our side.
- The physical reactions we label fear can be our ally if we begin to think of "racehorse nerves" and use that adrenaline to be our best.
- We will never be perfect, but we can be the best we can be at this moment. Aim for excellence.

Boyd and I let it intimidate me. I was also intimidated by the fact that my mentor, Charlie Cullen, had recommended me for the gig. I wanted Charlie to be proud he'd recommended me. Succeeding was terribly important to me. So important I was filled with fear.

On that day, my fear became my ally. My fear so motivated me that I was more effective than I'd ever been. Without understanding it at the time, I had transformed my fears into racehorse nerves. Into energy. Had I been too comfortable, my presentation would probably have been completely forgettable.

Fear became my ally.

In the next chapter, we'll look at how you can not only manage your fear, you can actually turn it into the most powerful tool in your toolbox—energy.

Calming Your Nerves

coach speaks

Experiment with what works best to calm your nerves. Here's what some of the pros do.

- As part of your preparation for your next presentation, take five minutes to imagine your worst-case scenario. Imagine that you forget everything. Imagine that you faint. Imagine your own worst nightmare. Spend five minutes in that nightmare and ask yourself this question: What will the results be? Will they fire you? Will you die? Will your spouse and kids stop loving you? Will you never work in this town again? Probably not. Most of us, when we spend five minutes with our worst nightmare, realize that we'll survive it. We'll be okay. Our careers won't be over. **People experience failure to one degree or another every day. They're alive, they survive and they thrive.** In fact, if you remember Ty's discussion on vulnerability in Chapter Three, you might actually discover that a nightmare presentation could have some unanticipated advantages. Audience members often connect in powerful ways when they realize we are human, too.

- Feed yourself some positive messages. "I know my subject well. I'm prepared and eager to give this audience what I have to share." "I'm glad I'm here and I'm going to enjoy this time with these people." And, as Ty said earlier, "So what?"

- Whenever Ty has a presentation to make, he spends the final moments before he begins mentally repeating a mantra: Energy. Energy. Energy. This takes his mind off the fear and places it on charging his batteries with the enthusiasm necessary for highly effective communication. What can your mantra be?

ENERGY :
THE HEARTBEAT OF YOUR PRESENTATION

Ch. 14

« Harness your passion and you become powerful. »

A friend and ESI graduate remembers making the connection between fear and energy.

She was speaking at a writer's conference attended by roughly two thousand people. Now, she knew her stuff. She was speaking on strong fictional characters, something she teaches regularly for one of her local colleges and at workshops all over the southeast. But this was big. This was San Francisco. Most folks would have the good sense to be scared witless.

"But I'd been through ESI," she says. "I knew I could do it. I knew the material. I knew the audience. I had no fear.

"And for the first time, I bombed."

She recalls that she immediately failed to connect with the audience. She couldn't get them interested in her subject, although it was a career-breaker for most of the unpublished authors in her audience. And the less they cared, the worse she got.

"It was the low point of my speaking career, no doubt about that. I haven't been asked to speak at the national conference again, and I can't say that I blame them."

What went wrong? She's a great teacher; she knew her material, felt confident. And, in fact, she decided in retrospect that was her biggest problem: She was too confident. No fear.

"I had no adrenaline. Nothing to kick in and turn into racehorse nerves. At that moment, all my ESI training kicked in except the connection between fear and energy. I was so calm I was complacent. The audience didn't know I was calm; all they picked up on was my complacence."

Remember our message from the last chapter: fear can

actually be transformed into one of our tools. In fact, used properly, it becomes one of our most powerful tools.

Fear, when managed, becomes energy.

Energy.

Energy is my mantra. I don't have a lucky tie or a medallion I keep in my hip pocket to remind me I can do it. The one thing I always carry with me is my awareness that energy is the key to reaching my audience. Energy is the number one power to have.

And you generate energy in two ways.

As my friend's story demonstrates, you generate it by successfully managing your fear.

And you generate it out of your passion for your topic.

Energy is every laugh we share with an audience of one or one hundred. Energy is all the things we didn't even have to put into words to convey. Energy is awareness of the moment, of the audience, of the message. And this awareness is not as keen when you're not somewhere on that continuum between panic and mild stress.

Energy is managed fear; energy is passion for your topic. Enthusiasm, fire in the belly. Energy is a tool you have absolute power to develop for yourself.

Energy is the heartbeat of every interaction, every communication, every presentation we share with another individual or group of individuals.

Passion: Find It, Feed It

If I could enforce one rule for anyone who ever makes a presentation, it would be this: Never speak about anything about which you have no passion.

The world's most powerful message delivered without energy, without passion, will fall unheard while the message delivered with passion or energy can change the world.

Every time I say this, people immediately remind me that there are a thousand times in a lifetime, especially in the business arena, when they believe they must speak about something for which they have no passion. Do you feel that way when you try to work up some enthusiasm for the things you speak about most often? Do you think: Who cares about the energy-efficiency rating of this refrigerator versus that one? Who cares whether this car has a V-6? Who cares whether the Board votes this month or next on EPA compliance? Who cares? Not me!

If the way you make your living has become so dull you can't work up some passion for what you do eight or ten hours a day, *it's time for a change!* If you're bored, you're boring.

But there's the mortgage. The car payment. The college fund. The little habit of three squares a day you'd hate to give up.

You can do one of two things when you realize you have no passion, and neither one necessarily requires you to give up the job.

You can find your passion.

Or you can feed your passion.

Find your passion. If you're doing something you hate, stop it. Discover what you love. Somebody makes a living at it, you can bet. And you can, too. Or, if changing careers isn't in the cards today, do the thing you love as a volunteer activity or as a hobby. But discover it and do it. When you do, you will be infused with enthusiasm for that subject. With passion. With energy.

And when that happens, that passion will spill over into all areas of your life.

If you are doing something with your leisure time that you are passionate about, every area of your life gives you more joy. Family, friends, work, every moment of your day, every activity in which you engage will feed your spirit. *Because as you feed your spirit, your spirit feeds the rest of your life.*

Find your passion. Stop and think about—not just in passing, but really put some concentration into this—what you'd want to be doing if you only had one year to live. If you suddenly won the lottery and could do whatever you wanted with your days. If you'd followed your heart when you were eighteen instead of following the money. What would it be? Then find a way to do it. Change jobs, if it's feasible, or invest your weekends in it or take an hour or two after work a couple of days a week. Begin to do the things that make your heart glad.

Lou Solomon, one of our ESI faculty, reminds us of a graduate whose experiences led him to a career path no one would have dreamed him capable of traversing.

Seems he was the kind of person others might have labeled a "computer geek." You know the type, quiet, shy, eyes on the ground, but so passionate about his subject that he rattled off information at ninety miles an hour. All those traits, unfortunately, meant he wasn't very good at communicating the wealth of information stored in his sharp mind.

Then he came to us for coaching. We taught him to add color and emotion to his communication, to slow down, to look people in the eye, to begin to connect with people when he spoke to them about computer technology, to communicate using both facts and feelings.

Afterward, this young man was asked to make a presentation at a convention in California, where his enthusiasm and knowledge were so impressive he was offered a job—doing presentations all over the country about the subject for which he had so much passion.

Find your passion.

That's one way to get the complacency out of your life. Here's the other:

Feed your passion.

What part of your message can you be passionate about? What sparks a glimmer of excitement in you for some small part of your message? Maybe you do sell cars for a living and you're sick of trying to get people excited over driver-side airbags when you know half of them don't have the means to buy anyway. Maybe you teach keyboarding skills to English as a Second Language students and it's beginning to grind on you. Maybe you've presented This Year's Budget Proposal so many years in a row you could do it in your sleep—and sometimes do. But moving on isn't an option.

If you aren't prepared to change the circumstances, change your attitude.

What can you be passionate about in your present circumstances? Can you begin to believe that your job isn't about driver-side airbags, but about helping each person who walks through the doors of the dealership find the best car for her circumstances, her checkbook? The car that will make her smile every time she gets in it? If you thought about that, instead of the last ten times you've made the same sales pitch, would it affect your level of enthusiasm?

If you thought of your job as changing other people's lives for the better instead of teaching keyboarding, for example, would that generate a little passion? Even teachers are in sales. They're selling the excitement of learning, the promise of a better tomorrow. Teachers sell dreams. How can we not be excited about that?

Maybe all you can say is: Today's presentation is not about me, it's about that great day when we drop my kid off at college, get her started on her dreams for the future. Can you picture that? Does that help? Can you picture the retirement home you and your spouse have in mind? That trip around the world you've been planning for years?

Does it help to keep your personal dreams in mind, and remember that what you're doing today is the next step toward the dream?

Focus on feeding whatever passion you can find in any circumstance you are in. Imagine that what you're saying can change a life—yours or your loved ones' or even a stranger's. Imagine the results of receiving the funding for this year's budget—not just dollars totaled up on a balance sheet, but the tangible results when those dollars are spent. The sheetrock lining someone's new home, or a sharp brochure that'll help some high school junior decide on a college, or new ergonomic chairs that'll make everybody in the office feel better at the end of the day and keep them off the chiropractor's table.

Can you get enthusiastic about those things? About people? About making a difference, even a very small difference, in somebody's life?

If necessary, the **why** becomes the key to your passion.

Find your passion or **feed** your passion. But bring that passion to your presentation however you must. Because without this one component—without enthusiasm, passion, energy—even the most powerful message can become trivial.

And with passion behind your message, even the most trivial message can become powerful.

Genuine Enthusiasm

An important part of the message of energy, then, is that your presentation must have two kinds of energy—physical energy and emotional energy, or passion.

Scientists understand that the world is made up of energy. Our world is as much energy as it is matter; in fact, some of today's best thinkers will tell you we are more energetic beings than physical beings. There is certainly no denying that

What is Energy?

Energy is:

- The laughter we share with others
- Emotions so powerful we don't even have to put them into words
- Being vitally present in this moment, for this audience, for this message
- Managed fear
- Enthusiasm, fire in the belly
- The heartbeat of every interaction we share with another person or group
- The unleashing of our genuine excitement

everything we see and feel can be measured in energy—including our presentations.

I've discovered that people get a little edgy when I talk to them about the energy in their presentations. They get a certain picture in their minds of what an energetic presentation looks like. And the picture in their minds is often negative.

What do you envision when I suggest that you bring more energy and enthusiasm to your presentations? Do you see yourself vigorously slapping people on the back? Talking fast and loud? Plastering a phony smile on your face, bounding onto the stage, a Rocky Balboa in a three-piece suit?

We've all seen those people. And cringed.

If that's energy, you might be thinking, count me out.

That's not energy. That's manufactured theatrics, not communication. True energy is never phony or inconsistent with our normal behavior.

Energy is the unleashing of our genuine excitement, for the message and for the audience. Passion and energy come in all kinds of forms. Some of the greatest energy is expressed on a pillow. In a whisper. Yes, sometimes in a shout. In a smile, a laugh, a wink.

One of the best examples of the infinite variety that goes into expressing passion can be found on the playing field. Compare FSU's flamboyant Bobby Bowden, for example, with the laid-back Tom Osborne from Nebraska. Think about video clips you might've seen of Tiger Woods each time he sinks a putt to win a major tournament. The leashed energy in his fist, the exuberance in his face as he all but roars? Now compare

Two Routes to Energy

Energy is the number one key to reaching your audience. You generate energy in two ways.

- Generate energy by successfully managing your fear.
- Generate energy out of your passion for your topic.

that image with Ben Crenshaw's 1995 win at the Masters, just after the death of his mentor, Harvey Penick. Crenshaw dropped his putter, buried his hands in his face and bent over, weeping, his emotions subdued yet overwhelmingly powerful. And because they were so powerful, he communicated them to everyone who saw him sink to his knees on the eighteenth green at Augusta.

Anyone who watched the 1998 Academy Awards presentations is unlikely to forget the moment when "Life Is Beautiful" was named Best Picture. Italian actor/director Roberto Benigni actually leaped over rows of seats to get to the front of the auditorium. Didn't all the viewers feel his sky-high emotions at that moment?

But we've also seen others choke back tears at powerful moments, and their restraint often fuels a strong response in us, as well.

Passion is displayed in countless ways. But it is always, always powerful.

Energy Thieves

If energy is one of our powerful allies when we present, we must learn to hunt down and destroy its enemies.

What are the enemies of energy? The saboteurs that rob us of our energy every time?

- **Burn-out for our subject matter**
- **Physical tiredness**
- **Complacency**
- **The unresponsive audience**

Let's talk about how to combat those energy thieves.

Burnout. How many times have you said the same thing? How many different ways can you find to convey the same message? How many times have you heard the same questions, the same responses?

Too many?

Repetition doesn't have to turn into burnout.

Update your talk with new anecdotes, with current references from the morning paper or the Internet, with new facts and statistics you collect at every opportunity.

The same message doesn't have to become the same talk. Talk from your heart instead of a script. Focus on the needs and interests of this specific audience instead of what you think you know about some generic, generalized audience. When you do, you'll find yourself giving a different presentation every time you speak.

Physical tiredness. We're all going to suffer from it from time to time. Sometimes, in fact, the better we get the more in demand we are and the more likely we are to run so hard we're often weary.

On more than one occasion, I've had presentations on the east coast and the west coast all in one day. I'd like to put my feet up at the end of a flight, not gear up for another presentation. Or I'd like to slide a little, give the second presentation a little less oomph than the first one. But the folks in L.A. don't care how well I did that morning in Manhattan. They want to see me at my best. They *deserve* to see me at my best.

If I'm on a particularly exhausting run, I owe it to myself and my audience to protect my energy level. So I rest on the flight, following all the best tips I know on reducing jet lag. I eat foods that metabolize more slowly—complex carbohydrates, for example, or foods that are a balance of protein and carbohydrates—so I don't hit a high, then quickly crash and burn. I go back to my hotel between sessions and put my feet up, listen to restful music, avoid the twenty calls I need to return until I've given the best I've got to the next audience. I like to carry a travel clock with me, so I can catnap soundly without the fear that I'll miss my "curtain call." I reduce aggravating situations as much as possible, and don't expend energy on petty annoyances.

Then, when it's time to present, I focus on rallying my energy. I remind myself I've only got an hour, or 20 minutes. And I give everything I have to that 20 minutes.

If, as speaking coach Roger Ayles says, I am the message, I do all I can to take care of this messenger. I protect the message by protecting the energy-level of the messenger.

Complacency. Some of the same solutions that work for burnout also work when we've become complacent. Staying fresh by constantly learning something new about our message. Adapting our presentations to the audience, the location, the circumstance.

A journalist friend tells me young reporters used to ask her how she remained interested in covering things like bond hearings or water-sewer board meetings month after month, year after year. She does it, she says, by looking for the human interest in the story. How will this mundane public meeting affect the people in the community? How will it affect the widow living on a fixed income or the parents struggling to keep the kids in shoes? If you focus on how the dry facts actually effect people, she says, there's no way to be bored, or boring.

I also avoid complacency by staying humble. I remind myself that Old Big Deal is truly not all that big a deal in the grand scheme of things. I remind myself that this audience is special. They have come to see me at my very best and most effective and they deserve nothing less. I remind myself that this moment is the only one I have. I may never have another opportunity to reach these people with this message. In truth, I may never have another chance to reach anyone with any message.

This moment is it. This moment is the most important one in my life. This moment is the only one I can live in.

When I remember that, it's hard to feel complacent.

The unresponsive audience. We've all had them. It's eight a.m. the day after a late-night session and they're more focused on the cup of coffee in their hands than anything you're saying. Or it's two p.m. after a business lunch of all-you-can-eat pasta and maybe a martini or two. They're yawning.

They're checking their watches. They're flipping through the agenda to see what's coming up.

You're gonna hate hearing this, but the problem is not the audience. The problem is not how little sleep they had or how much lunch they devoured.

A friend, Kevin, leads adult Sunday school classes at his church. Here's how he says it: "In order to pull that passion out of the group, I have to have that passion myself."

I always know I'm not at top form by the general lethargy of the audience. *Because they follow my lead.* Certainly a p.m. time slot can be more challenging than an a.m. slot, when people are more fresh. But if I give my audience something to be excited about, they will follow me, they will forget their coffee or their watch, even the plane they have to catch. There are very few bad audiences, just poorly prepared or dull presenters.

Harness Your Passion

If I could teach you only one thing it would be to harness your passion. To direct it into your words, your actions, your facial expressions. Make full use of your energy and enthusiasm. Harness your passion and you become powerful.

But tapping into your passion and making it work for you cannot be taught. It is not something I can train you into doing. It is not something that can be gained by practicing or memorizing.

Energy, passion, enthusiasm are the territory of the heart, of the spirit.

If you have stifled that spirit, ignored it, denied it, you have limited yourself. You have made yourself infinitely poorer. If you have bored your spirit into submission, you have robbed yourself of the opportunity to make the most of every moment you have on this earth.

I can't change any of that for you. But you can change it.

You can accept the challenge to step out of the box you've

built for yourself. You can open yourself to reinvigorating your spirit. You can find the thing that gets your blood pumping, the thing you want to share with the world.

And if you already know that territory well, if you've already found your passion and are now ready to unleash it on the world, using the tools in your toolbox—well, allow me to step back.

Go change your world.

Maximizing Your Energy

coach speaks

Energy is both contagious and attractive. Two people the same age can create such a different reaction in people simply because of their energy level. One fifty-year-old may appear ready to climb Mount Everest, while another may look two steps away from pushing up daisies. And the only difference will be their level of energy.

How do we maximize our energy level? Here are a few tips that have worked for us and others over the years.

- **PUT IT IN WRITING.** If you carry note cards or other materials with you when you present, remind yourself of this in your notes, also: Energy. Write it on your note cards. Put it on sticky-notes and attach it to the top of your stack of hand-outs. Red-ink it into the margins of the report you've brought to quote from. Pencil it lightly along the edges of your flip chart. Energy.

- **REPEAT, REPEAT, REPEAT.** Repeat the message to yourself as you're being introduced. "Energy! Energy! Energy!" Your body and your mind will get the message.

- **STAND UP.** Unless there's a rule against standing, get on your feet. Even if it's a small group. Even if others who are presenting have remained in their seats, tell them you want to stand. Find a plausible reason to stand. Standing both generates energy and radiates power.

Ch. 15 WALKING WITH GIANTS

« Every time you use one of your tools...you become a little taller...little more powerful. »

Your toolbox is well-stocked.

No matter where you started, you now have tools you didn't have fourteen chapters ago. In fact, you now have every tool I own, every tool owned by friends and colleagues of mine who are among the most powerful and successful presenters in the world—members of the National Speakers Association and the Speakers' Roundtable.

Like them, you now own a Million-Dollar Toolbox, stocked with all the essentials for powerful communication. When we started this journey, I told you we'd share them with you, introduce them to you one-by-one, with practical tips for putting them to work. And we have.

- You've learned the ten deadly distractions that make any speaker less effective, and the skills that shut down those distractions.

- You have some practice tools for discovering your own authentic style.

- You've learned how to find your common ground with any audience—of one or one thousand—as well as how to make quick connections under any circumstances.

- You've learned ways to listen more effectively, how to tolerate—and put to work—silences, how to give clear signals that you're listening.

- You've learned how to get comfortable with the actor's tools of eye contact, smiles, varied facial expressions, purposeful movement and effective gestures.

- You've learned how to expand your comfort zone so you can unleash the authentic you, no longer bound by false notions of professionalism.

- You've learned to play the voice you were born with, using the tools of breath, projection, diction and vocal variety.

- You've learned how to organize an effective presentation, as well as how to create powerful opening and closing statements.

- You've learned effective techniques for rehearsal, how to own the territory wherever and whenever you speak, how to handle Q-and-A sessions, even ways to disarm a hostile audience.

- You've learned the truth about fear, relaxation techniques for managing it, and how to turn that fear into your ally.

- You've learned the power of finding and feeding your passion.

I promised you a million-dollar toolbox, and the truth is I believe the tools you now own are worth far more than that. The tools you now own are personal and professional relationship skills you weren't fully aware of before. You now have the tools to be successful in any area of your life, because that is what the ability to communicate effectively can do for you.

These tools enable you to communicate effectively in all areas of your life, at work, at home, with friends, in your leisure or civic activities.

The value of communicating well cannot be measured in dollars and cents.

And it's all there, in your toolbox.

But the biggest difference in your presentation skills, the real strides in your ability to communicate effectively, come next. Come when you close this book, when you put it on the shelf with all the other books you've accumulated over the years in your search for a better life, a better career, a better you.

What's it going to be?

Are you going to put this book up there on the shelf with vague promises that you'll try that stuff from Ty Boyd sometime? Are you going to go back out there and wing it the next time you make a presentation? Are you going to assume that this audience is the same as the last one and needs no additional preparation? Are you going to get stuck behind that lectern, with your written speech and your hands in your pockets and be satisfied with a bunt because you aren't willing to take the risk and swing for the fence?

Some people do that, of course. Their career path often reflects that decision—dramatically.

And others decide to walk with the giants.

I walk with giants every day. And I don't just mean the men and women who sit with me around the Speakers' Roundtable, that elite group of professional speakers I am honored to rub elbows with. I mean women and men just like you—sales reps and marketing execs and investment counselors and church elders and family breadwinners. People who walked away from presentation training and put their new tools to work in their lives.

Those men and women became giants.

So can you.

But not if you put the book on the shelf and forget it.

Open Your Toolbox

When we finish our three-day Excellence in Speaking Institute, one of our top instructors, Cam Marston, leaves our graduates with this thought: "You're now able to change what people think by what you do. Have you got the courage to open your toolbox?"

That, of course, is the key. Opening the toolbox. Pulling out your tools, one by one, and using them every chance you get. Practicing them. Honing them. Becoming proficient in their use.

Right this minute, you're probably saying, "Well, sure, Ty, but I don't get all that many opportunities to present to an audience."

But I want to remind you that if you only think these tools are applicable when you're assigned to speak for a group, you're missing about 90 percent of their value.

All of us—you and I—speak to the public every day. Some days, our public is our children, our spouse, our boss, our co-workers, our employees, our customers. Some days, the event that will demand the most of our skills is as simple as getting our point across to the car dealership mechanic.

Every day, in every way, we communicate. Do it well. Do it effectively. Use your tools.

Believe it or not, every time you use one of your tools and see it work, you become a little taller. You become a little more confident, a little more powerful. You are walking the path of giants. And when you walk in their company often enough, you become one of them.

One of our graduates, Douglas Snell from Ephrata, Pennsylvania, let us know recently that his efforts to improve his communications skills had results he'd never anticipated.

"Ty's training helped me at home, with eye contact with my family—we communicate very effectively now," Doug says. "At work, making presentations, I never fail, being able to reach into that 'toolbox' of skills Ty taught us. Further, it has helped me with volunteer organizations, where I have been very effective in communicating a need.

"And many times I have to think on my feet. This is probably the most effective tool I learned about. I get questioned many times and now feel very confident knowing how to think on my feet...I find myself using gestures, arm motion, facial expression—even a smile...Oh, I still have my moment (of fear) before I begin, but I hear the voices of Ty and the other instructors encouraging me...and immediately my fear is gone."

Doug says so well what so many others have told us. That better communication pays off in profound ways in every area of their lives.

And you can do what Doug does. You can remember me speaking to you when you are tempted to give in to fear or an unwillingness to feel phony or to interrupt instead of listening. Imagine the coach on your shoulder. Take me with you. Invite Pat along.

Open your toolbox.

I see it over and over. People see themselves for the first time in a different light. They go out enormously repaired, filled with self-worth. What happens is much more than learning to be an efficient communicator. It's learning to be a whole person, no longer wrapped up in Be Perfect or straight-jacketed by the narrow boundaries of our comfort zone.

The skills you've packed away in your toolbox have the power to free you. The power to set your life on fire with new passion for its possibilities.

That's why people get so emotional about learning presentation skills. It's not so much packing your toolbox with some practical skills. It's because their self-worth quotient goes way up. Learning to be a powerful communicator is about self-empowerment.

Self-empowerment.

That is a million-dollar tool, don't you agree?

Thank you for letting us share this journey with you. Thank you for your willingness to become a better communicator in a world where technology all too often replaces true communication. Thank you for becoming an ambassador for dialoguing, not monologuing. Thank you for listening.

Now get out there and use your toolbox.

And drop us a line now and then to let us know how it's going.